CULTIVATING MINDS TO OWN THYSELF

BY JAMEEL DAVIS

COVER DESIGN: Kevin Conwell Jr.

PAGE DESIGN: Rhonda Crowder and Associates, LLC.

EDITOR: Rhonda Crowder and Associates, LLC.

PUBLISHER: ElevatedWaves Publishing Company

ISBN-13: 978-0-692-89211-4 | ISBN-10: 0-692-89211-7

Table of Contents

Table of Contents

First and foremost, we thank the creator for another day of life. Despite where we are in our lives, the struggles and successes we have experienced, He brought us back here again and together. The gift of life is the greatest gift of all and nothing else truly matters, except the love you receive from those who matter the most.

Foreword

Every moment is an opportunity to become a better YOU, to make a difference, to fall, to get back up, to rise, to fall again, to rise right back up and to be the best YOU that you can be.

— JAMEEL DAVIS

4-19-2015: "Thank you Andre for your support." This short and precise message precedes Mr. Jameel Davis's signature in the inside cover of his first book *How Success Became My Focus.* At first glance to anyone pursuing my personal library, this message would not suggest that Jameel and I are kindred spirits; peers, young Black Kings that are forever tied together through several important vines of life. Instead, it is more of a motif of Jameel's spirit and the energy he chooses to emit. Jameel doesn't waste. I knew from the time he offered me the opportunity to write the foreword for this book, that none of my time would be wasted reading his prudent and conversant opinions and narrative.

If you are like me, your favorite song on one of your favorite albums will change from time to time based on your mood, experiences, and coordinates in your current life. Cultivating Minds to Own Thyself is a lot like your favorite album. Your favorite chapter will change from time to time as you explore your true identity, purposes, motivation and academic history.

At the time of this foreword, my favorite chapter is the first one: "Define, Identify and Accept Thyself." The title is a deliberate reminder that we are all one-of-one, a true masterpiece from a greater power, (a power I personally acknowledge as my Lord and Savior). From the time we are born, one of the very first gifts we receive is our name. Jameel pushes and responsibly challenges us to explore exactly who we are past what the world and others give us as our identity Professionally, I am in the field of Outpatient Physical Therapy. Many of our patients are given instructions, literature and pictures to remind them of proper form, posture and exercise techniques. This book is an asset I'll keep in my library because it is a reminder for me to have the proper intellect and drive in matters of thyself as an entrepreneur and as a leader, this book helps me keep my internal compass properly calibrated.

Jameel's character pedigree is inspirational in itself. I've known Jameel for more than 15 years through our strongest vine – our mentor Mr. Leon R. Anderson III. Success initially was the main branch of our vine through Mr. Anderson. Jameel (even through a few years younger than me) earned better grades than me in high school and he is unknowingly, partly responsible for my collegiate grades improving. Now that we have both had a taste of what the world says success is, we have found ourselves using our talents (both God given and those that we cultivated) to dig deeper for more.

Even though, I do not always personally agree with every opinion and point of view Jameel has, there has never been a lack of respect for his position. As previously stated, "Jameel doesn't waste." He stays true to his spirit by systematically defying and rejecting just one sole source of information. Both anecdotal and objective material formulates his thoughts, unlike unreliable energies such as emotion.

Jameel has earned every opportunity and blessing to come his way.

Through all of his outlets (this book included), he sincerely wishes to share with the world his journey: successes, triumphs, failures and setbacks with the hope that it will pave the path for the next queen and/or king. I've watched Jameel lead and follow, a characteristic that I personally look for in every leader. His work with the Cleveland Renaissance Movement is an illustration of his ability to add value while following the lead. The latest branch of our vine that we are connected to which is fatherhood, strongly shows his leadership as a father to Jaheir. I am the proud father of Anderson Kaiser Russell. Jameel and I have had countless conversations on why it's so important to lead our children. I see Jameel's maturation and leadership in every page of this book.

Truly inspired after reading Jameel's second book, I purposely did not include any sources or outside information for the creation of this foreword. I wanted to let my spirit and heart speak as I have accepted the challenge to cultivate my mind to own thyself. I strongly believe that if you can even absorb the equivalent of a mustard seed of information, inspiration and drive from this book, it will not take very long before you garner positive results. Jameel is aggrandizing success by inviting us to find success with significance through our most powerful personal asset – our minds.

Create Wealth and Inspire, *Andrè R. Russell*

Introduction

CULTIVATING MINDS TO OWN THYSELF

"In the introduction of On Becoming A Leader, Warren Bennis stated, "On Becoming A Leader is based on the assumption that leaders are people who are able to express themselves fully. By this I mean that they know who they are, what their strengths and weaknesses are, and how to fully deploy their strengths and compensate for their weaknesses. They also know what they want, why they want it, and how to communicate what they want to others in order to gain their cooperation and support. Finally, they know how to achieve their goals." He further communicated, the key to full self-expression is understanding one's self and the world, and the key to understanding is learning from one's own life and experience.

From that moment, *Cultivating Minds to Own Thyself* was born. Reading Warren Bennis's introduction, inspired me to write this book, with the intentions of helping young black men and women discover their purpose and to take ownership of their lives without using society's standards.

It was almost six years ago when I decided to turn the light bulb on in my head. I awakened myself to take control of my life to become self-knowledgeable, self-disciplined, self-determined, self-educated and to become the man most people would love to be around and to reach my full potential. Since then, I have witnessed many people destroy their life by accepting to be controlled by the negative influences of others. Many are now lost in an environment filled with valuable opportunities for growth. They have been influenced to walk in circles. They have no direction, settling for lack. Those individuals have been miseducated and misguided by the lack of education, miseducation, and direction from their parents and elders, by the poisoned images on the television screen, by the poisoned messages flowing through the radio frequencies, through their headphones and into their ears. Negative energy created to control and destroy the mind in order for the dominant society to conquer.

My turning point in life came about when I visited the Black Holocaust Museum in Philadelphia, Pennsylvania, which was about five years ago. Inside the museum, there was a room filled with obituaries from all individuals who have been killed by BOB (Black on Black Violence) in the neighborhoods of Philly. The owner/instructor shared stories of the homicides and really encouraged me to open my eyes and to begin treating my brothers and sisters fairly and to protect them. The spirits of the hundreds of black individuals who were on the walls in the museum, entered my soul and woke up a part of me which made me change my negative thinking toward others. Those stories and the spirits of the individuals in the museum weren't the only things that had a huge impact on my life. The room with the obituaries also had a coffin in the center of it. Upon sharing the stories of the many individuals killed from black violence, the instructor instructed me to open the coffin and to look inside. Not knowing what to expect, uncontrollably scared and nervous, I looked inside and I saw myself. I stared at myself for several minutes, very emotional, and in deep thought. I then said to myself that, "if I continue to act negatively toward others, especially toward my own kind, this could be me." I said, "I have to make a change. A change in myself and in others." I decided at that moment, when I was looking at my reflection in the coffin, to be the change I wanted to see among my peers, my community and throughout the world. I told myself, "I'm going to take control of my life, become the man many people would love to be around, achieve positive goals and reach my full potential."

As I look in the mirror today, I see the controller of my life, a role model to all, a compassionate educator and leader, a respectful and loving man, who have become the change he wished to see nearly six years ago. Looking at the obituaries on the walls and looking into a coffin to only see myself was the wakeup I needed to become a successful, educated individual and to develop love for all humanity.

While writing this book, I had the opportunity to dialogue with Dorian W. and Kenta S., and many other individuals who were housed in the County Corrections Center in Cleveland, Ohio. I shared my story of how I use to be the person others wanted me to be up until my junior year at Kent State University, when I decided to reinvent myself, express myself the way I wanted to and become the person I wanted to become. I explained to them fully, how I had to get rid of the negative influences surrounding me: family, peers, music, television etc. in order for me to reach my full potential. I mentioned to Dorian and Kenta that, those who you think will be there for you, won't be there when you need them most. Dorian and Kenta then asked, "how did I determine which people to eliminate from my circle?" and I said, "When you go to court, look behind you. Those are the people who got your back. Those who have been enjoying the fruits of your labor, who isn't there to support you in times of need are the ones you clear from your circle. Those who do not uplift you and inspire you, but bring you down and discourage you are the ones you get rid of immediately. You should have people that empower you, support you, and who get out of your way on your team. That is how they will get the best of you and how you will get the best of yourself."

Brothers and sisters, think of your brain as a garden, you must lay rich soil, plant good seeds, water it, keep animals and weeds out in order to blossom healthy plants, fruits, and vegetables. You have to plant positive thoughts in your mind in order to develop into the successful person you wish to become. Negativity is the cause of disease, destruction, and disaster. Positivity results in production. The goal is to eliminate negativity from your subconscious mind, so you can enjoy a lifetime of happiness and joy. With negativity erased from your subconscious mind, your vision becomes clear and you will have room to take control of your life and to fully express yourself, maximizing your strengths and achieving your goals.

I don't have a coffin or hundreds of obituaries here for you to look at to encourage you to become your best self and to make a difference.

However, I do have this book, *Cultivating Minds to Own Thyself*, which will have an even greater impact on you and which will definitely encourage you to define, identify, and accept yourself without using society's standards. This book will also encourage you to modify your thoughts, so you can become your best self and to make a difference in the lives of others.

This book was birthed so that you can take full control of your life. You will learn about the miseducation, the true meaning of education, financial literacy, the affect that bad parenting has on children, the effects of good parenting, relationships, effective dating, getting rid of negative tendencies from your subconscious mind, treating others fairly and putting all your situations in the hands of the Creator. All are important for taking ownership of your life and becoming the successful individual you are destined to become.

I took it upon myself to educate myself on the subjects I will discuss in this book. All information enclosed is based off life experiences, except brief quotations and summaries of those featured within.

What's stopping you from revealing your true self to yourself and those who matter? What's hiding under those layers of skin, under that foundation?

Chapter One

DEFINE, IDENTIFY & ACCEPT THYSELF

"No one can teach you how to be yourself, to take charge, to express yourself, EXCEPT YOU"

— WARREN BENNIS

Identity is the consciousness of our true nature," says Dr. Na'im Akbar, author of *Know Thy Self*. He also says, in order to become really human, our humanity must be educed, brought forth or brought out. To be human, he continued, however implies consciousness or awareness of who and what we are.

Author of *On Becoming A Leader*, Warren Bennis says, to "know thyself means separating who you are and what you want to be from what the world thinks and wants you to be."

To know yourself would be to know such things as your deepest thoughts, desires, and emotions, your character traits, your values, what makes you happy and why you think and do the things you think and do, said the writer of *Know Thy Self - Really*, Quassim Cassam.

Dr. Akbar explains the earliest step in the educational process and how that step is an important part of our identity. The earliest step in the educational process is selecting a name. The name comes to symbolize the much broader reality of identity. It is with the name that we become identified among the human community and within the name is a full range of dimensions of our identity… The name usually identifies the family or direct teachers from whom we come. The language of the name tells us much about our nationality, native tongue, culture, history and a wide range of things about our human social function and origin.

For example, the name Ashani originates in one of the African languages and means "aggressive, warlike." It is the name of a region in Ghana, as well as the name of the major ethnic group in Ghana. The name Ayo originates in African languages and means "full of joy." It can be used as both feminine and masculine given names. It is mainly used in Nigeria. The Judeo-Christian name Abdiel means "servant of God." It is known as being the name of the faithful seraph who withstood Satan when he urged the angels to revolt in 17th Century English Poet John Milton's epic "Paradise Lost." The Judeo-Christian name Aldebaran derives from Arabic, meaning "follower." Aldebaran is also the name of the brightest stars in the constellation Taurus, presumably so named because it appears to follow the Pleiades rightward across the night sky. The Islamic name Dafeenah, which is a female name that originated from the Pakistani and Indian language Urdu, means "hidden treasure." The Islamic name Aynulhayat, which also originated from the Pakistani and Indian language Urdu, means "spring (fountain) of life."

Your name should hold a detailed meaning of who you are, your origin, culture, and character traits. My son's mother named him Jaheir. Jaheir is always used as a boy's name in England and Wales.

Upon conducting a little research of the meaning of Jaheir, I found that his name means, to be honest, benevolent, brilliant, and often inventive, full of high inspirations. He is courageous, honest, determined, original, and creative. He is a leader, especially for a cause. Sometimes, he does not care to finish what he starts and may leave details to others. He does well in a position of authority and prospers in intellectual and professional fields.

Jaheir is bold, independent, inquisitive, and interested in research. He knows what he wants and why he wants it. He will find the best contentment in life when he owns his own home and provide well for his family and loved ones. He will have a great sense of responsibility and duty. He is comforting, appreciative, and affectionate. His obligation in life is to hold justice and truth and, if he follows the law, he can find the great happiness and satisfaction.

It is my duty to teach him when he becomes of age, the meaning of his name so he can live out his purpose. Some of the characteristics mentioned above, I already see in him at age four. He's independent, has a great sense of responsibility and duty. He is comforting, appreciative, and affectionate.

It is within the name that should tell us about our family and our defined purpose in life. It's important that we know who we are, not only to be accepted among the human race but to continue the advancement of our family, culture, history, and native tongue.

While in a black studies course at Kent State University, I learned about the Nature of Definition. It states, "Once an individual's definition of himself is the same as that of the oppressor than the oppressor can destroy that individual without physical stress." That means, once an individual, group, or society wrongly define and label you, you begin to believe, accept, and act accordingly to the title/class they assign.

Miseducation begins at the level where the person is taught an alien identity and nothing about their true identity. They learn to see themselves in someone else's story and do not learn about their own story, says Dr. Akbar. For instance, we black folks have been led to think we are too fat, too skinny, too dark, too light, too short, too tall and ugly. During slavery, we were made fun of and criticized by whites for our natural given features. They said our hair was nappy, our nose was too large, our lips were too big, and that we had large eyes and ugly teeth. They said we look and act like monkeys. The slave era prevented many of us from exploring our true talents, gifts, and beauty. Over all, slavery made us look down upon ourselves and upon one another mainly because we were in captivity.

Four plus centuries of the dehumanization of our black ancestors resulted in majority of us today looking in the mirror and becoming upset by what we see. It resulted in the belittlement and criticizing of each other. Our oppressors have miseducated us. Our ancestors were never told they were handsome and beautiful, but instead they heard the words ugly and filthy. Slave owners turned us against one another: light-skin versus dark-skin, men versus women, educated versus uneducated, good hair versus bad hair, field versus house slaves, tall versus short, fat versus slim and so forth.

Generations after generations, we have experienced dehumanization from our oppressors and now we do it to ourselves without them having to do anything. The disease has been planted in our cells. Today, some of our people wear hair extensions and get relaxers, because they believe their natural hair is ugly and nappy. They don't appreciate the strong and pretty hair the creator has blessed them with. Because our ancestors were told that their hair was ugly and nappy during the slave era, men mixed potatoes, lard and lye (a strong alkaline solution used for cleaning and washing) together, creating the first relaxer which burned their scalp. They wanted to have straight hair like their slave masters. They hated their natural appearance. They used axle grease to lay down their hair and used it to dye their gray hair black. Today, we are ashamed of our gray hair, so we dye it black.

Our Black women learned that, heat straightened hair and used the iron to straighten their hair. They twisted their hair with yarn to keep it untangled. They used sulfur to treat parasites in their hair and washed their hair with dishwater to moisturize it. Cornmeal was used to dry clean their hair. Today, many of our Black women use all sorts of chemicals and products on their hair, taking them further and further away from their natural culture.

During the 1890's, Madam CJ Walker suffered from a scalp ailment (illness) that caused her to lose some of her hair. Walker later invented, Madam Walker's Wonderful Hair Grower, a scalp conditioning and healing formula. She went on to invent the first official hair relaxer and a line of other African American hair products, making her the first black American woman to become a self-made millionaire.

Today, doctors have found black rings around the brain of black women when they perform autopsies. Research suggests the black rings are from the hair chemicals the women have placed in their hair over the course of their life. Many believe the chemicals may have contributed to their death.

Many of my people apply makeup/foundation to lighten their skin because they believe brown doesn't seem to glow. Because our Black ancestors were told their skin was ugly, they would lighten their skin to look like their Caucasian slave-owners, who was said to be the beautiful ones. We don't appreciate our dark and light skin with that good ole melanin in it that protects us from UV radiation. The skin that many other races admire.

Most of us dislike our lips and nose, and are getting plastic surgery because we've been told our lips and nose are too big. We are afraid to be our natural self because we believe we will be made fun of, picked on and criticized.

The reason why I mentioned historical facts about hair and skin tone is so we can grow to learn and love our natural self. We must know where we come from as a people, so we know where to go in the future.

Many of us define ourselves by having fancy or luxury material items and, once we acquire all the items we desire, we still find ourselves unhappy I believe it's because we limit our image, education, and success to social standards: having long straight hair, straight white teeth, being slim in size, having designer clothes and shoes, obtaining a degree from a college or university, having a high paying job, nice cars, a big house, jewelry etc.

I believe one must limit their image, education and success to their own liking. One must be able to define, identify, and accept thyself, their education and success without using social standards. Success to me is achieving all that you desire without violating the rights of anyone else. Success also means, if you manage to get to your level of contentment, you must send the elevator back down and help someone else reach the top.

You don't have to have all the money in the world, fancy cars, clothes, jewelry and a big fancy house to be successful. Success is what you make it.

In order to define ourselves, we must first search deep within ourselves to find our own purpose, passion, and desires. If that becomes difficult, engage in activities that bring you joy and happiness as well as activities that are challenging.

These activities will help you determine your strengths and weakness, which are part of self-definition. Be willing to step out of your comfort zone and take risk towards change. Taking risks will help you reveal a part of you that you didn't know you had.

We should see ourselves achieving our own set of goals and becoming who we want to be in life. Fulfilling someone else's purpose and desires makes us artificial and it makes it harder for us to be recognized and to stand out. After visualizing ourselves maximizing our full potential, living in our purpose and obtaining our own desires, we must then create a plan to accomplish them and begin at once, using faith and effort.

I participated in a writing contest where I was asked to define what it means to have beauty and brains? Although I did not win the contest, I still believe I had a great idea of what it means. I defined what it meant to me without using society's standards as being rich in mind, body and in spirit. Being rich in mind is being able to identify yourself without using your government issued name and social security number, being able to define your purpose and desires, and communicating those desires to others. Being rich in mind is being self-determined, disciplined, responsible, and having good decision-making skills. Having neither an identity nor a purpose and being indecisive are harmful to the growth of self and our civilization. A person that does not know himself/herself is subject to being controlled by everyone other than themselves. They will fall for anything because they have nothing to stand up for.

Napoleon Hill stated, "The most common weakness of all human beings is the habit of leaving their minds open to the negative influences of other people." Leaving your mind open to the negative influences of others results in negative tendencies being applied to the subconscious mind and those tendencies transferring to your physical being.

Negative tendencies which could be applied to the subconscious mind include hatred, jealousy, envy, and selfishness. A rich-minded individual would only allow positive tendencies to impact their subconscious mind which will transfer into their physical being. A rich minded individual knows that having a negative attitude towards others will not foster success. Being rich in mind also means reaching a decision not to worry about what people think say or do. He and she can withstand and handle criticism.

One of the things I face as a writer is criticism from non-writers who lack reading comprehension skills and who cannot dissect the information that I present. Although, the messages written are universal to all in efforts of helping us become better than yesterday. I am a writer who does not feed into the destructiveness of outsiders and think ahead to accomplish even greater things. The ability to ignore is my greatest gift and is one of the foundations of my current success.

There are too many people in the world to make explanations to. Part of being an adult is expressing yourself fully, without having to explain any decision you make to anyone. Part of that process is ignoring those who do not matter and who isn't beneficial to your growth.

Health and fitness go hand and hand when forming a rich body. Providing your body with adequate food, nutrition, rest and exercise, to protect each of the body's eleven systems: Circulatory, Digestive, Endocrine, Immune, Lymphatic, Muscular, Nervous, Reproductive, Respiratory, Skeletal, and Urinary system is what I consider being rich in body. In order to have a beautiful body, you don't have to have a six pack, strong muscular arms, large breast or a huge buttock. Eating healthy food and partaking in daily routine exercises are all that's necessary to have a beautiful body. A healthy diet and exercise will provide you with a good amount of energy when engaging in some of your favorite activities.

If you are able to wake up each morning, look in the mirror and say, "I love you" without applying makeup or foundation, grooming your hair and dressing in your day clothes, you have a beautiful body. Being able to accept yourself, your physical features, and your interior, shows you are rich in mind and in body.

Many people often find themselves putting on this image of someone else, to attract those who do not deserve them. They spend hundreds or even thousands of dollars keeping up with fashion trends: hair, designer clothes, bags, shoes etc.; to impress those who do not matter. All the time and effort invested in keeping up with trends could be invested in finding yourself.

When you have found yourself, you wouldn't think twice about what everyone else is doing and you wouldn't have to worry about impressing others because you would be living to impress yourself. True beauty is developing your own style and being able to identify yourself without luxury items, designer clothes, shoes, makeup/foundation and money. .

The ability to create and maintain positive energy, and being able to use it to inspire others to become greater than yesterday, is what I call having a rich spirit. For me, the best part of waking up is knowing someone is waiting for me to change their life. Doing right by all of the Creator's creations without thinking twice about it is also what I call having a rich spirit. Also, known as having positive tendencies applied to the subconscious mind and transferred into its physical being.

It is highly important that we set aside our anxieties, come out from our shells and establish an identity of our own. Akbar reminds us that, in the process of miseducation, we have learned the proper aesthetic (or standard of beauty) is the European Caucasian aesthetic and anything else is deficient. Something as simple as the appearance of the toys we play with or the characters in the story books begin to teach us this aesthetic. For African and Hispanic children, Barbie dolls, GI Joe and fairy tales should look like them. Knowing who we are is essential for demanding acceptance in society.

"A part of our self-respect and dignity is acquired through the input of ideas from our environments. We have to be exposed to images that mirror ourselves which are worthy of dignity and worthy of respect. The African child, who never sees African people who are respectable and dignified, has difficulty learning to respect the part of themselves that they recognize as being like Africans. If the only human images that are presented to them in their education are images of dignified people who are not Africans, then they have difficulty finding mirrors of themselves in their education," says Dr. Akbar. "People can only belong to themselves if their identity is an outgrowth of their history, culture, reality and survival needs."

Here's a self-assessment exercise for you:

Every morning, enter your bathroom or somewhere in your home where there's a mirror (a full body mirror is perfect).

Before applying makeup/foundation, grooming your hair, brushing your teeth and putting on clothes, look in the mirror for a minute or two and repeat, "I love you for who you are and I refuse to be controlled by what others think, say and do" then smile.

The purpose of this exercise is to get you to love yourself and to free yourself. Many people spend time trying to fit in with society or trying to live up to someone else's standards instead of their own. Loving yourself and refusing to be deployed by the thoughts and actions of others helps you become self-disciplined and it helps you to live out your purpose. When given the chance to identify yourself, give your own definition of yourself. Let others know how you perceive yourself and show them that you have ownership of your life. If not, they will decide and control your life for you.

> "Beauty is beyond skin deep and skin can tear very easily, damaging that beautiful face. But a solid core, a solid core will override every exterior aspect you have - your breasts, buttocks, tattoos, piercings, cosmetics, jewelry, clothes, shoes, etcetera. A cleansed and solid interior is way more attractive than anything that lies on the surface of your skin. That solid foundation will help you attract everything you desire."

> — *JAMEEL DAVIS*

> "To change anything on the outside, you must become the change on the inside. How the change will happen on

the outside is not up to you. That is the job of the Universe. Your job is to radiate all good from the inside and the outside circumstances will change to reflect the 'all good' inside you."

— RHONDA BYRNE "The Secret"

"One of the biggest mistakes people make in life is spending their life attempting to please those who do not matter. You should spend life doing things you enjoy. Don't allow yourself to be deployed by what people think, say, or do, DEPLOY YOURSELF."

— JAMEEL DAVIS

"Only by much searching and mining are gold and diamonds obtained, and man can only find everything truth connected with his being, if he will dig deep into the mind of his soul, that he is the maker of his character, the molder of his life, and the builder of his destiny. He may unerringly prove, if he will watch, control, and alter his thoughts, tracing their effects upon himself, upon others, and upon his life."

— JAMES ALLEN

I AM WHO I AM

Society and others don't define who I am I have my own definition of self and, therefore, anything you or anyone say regarding my identity can't change the fact that I am who I am.

I cannot and will not argue with you to change your opinion about me, because I am who I am.

Your opinion of me is your own opinion and the only thing that matter is my own opinion of self because I am who I am.

The important decisions I make in life are decided based upon my own instincts and, therefore, I will not allow anyone to make them for me because I am who I am.

What others think say or do will not deploy me. I will deploy myself because I am who I am.

— JAMEEL DAVIS

Behind every layer of skin on a person's body, typically their face, there's a different tone of color. Which means, every time you wipe off foundation or peel off a piece of skin, you reveal a different part of you - a part that you may not want the world to see. Peel off your shirt and you are left with your bare chest. Beneath your chest, you have something that's called your "core," which holds your true being. Tap into your core and reveal your true self, not only to the world around you but to yourself.

If you don't find who you are, it will be very difficult for you to learn about anyone else and be receptive of all the benefits they have to offer. A person may not reveal certain parts of them to you or give you their all because you are covered in layers of foundation, with artificial eyelashes, mascara/makeup, eyeliner, lipstick, false hair, tattoos, gold teeth, etc. and are hiding under sunglasses and hats, which aren't revealing the true you. We expect others to reveal their true colors but hold on tight to ours, living a lie that's covered with glitter.

If you find yourself, become true to yourself and believe in yourself, you wouldn't have to live your life playing hide and seek, or trying hard to be accepted. People aren't accepted by the nature of their exterior skin but by the solid core in which they have inside. Once you accept who you truly are, that's all the acceptance you need. When those of interest see that strength and self-acceptance they may be willing to reveal more of them to you.

— JAMEEL DAVIS

Chapter Two

BECOME YOUR OWN EDUCATIONAL INSTITUTION

"If God had meant man to fly, he would have given him wings.

But the Wright Brothers disagreed and built an airplane."

— WARREN BENNIS

To own thyself means inventing yourself, expressing yourself fully, taking control of yourself, your own life, using yourself completely to reach your full potential and to make your dreams come true. Not anyone else's.

Abraham Maslow, author of *Father Reaches of Human Nature*, says, when becoming ourselves, we must listen to the impulse voices. Many of us listen not to ourselves but to mommy's introjected voice or daddy's voice or the voice of the establishment, of the elders, of authority, or of tradition. Far too often, we have many parents and or guardians, teachers, and pastors, choosing their child(ren)'s future instead of showing them how or even allowing them to fulfill their own dreams and desires. They instruct their children to go to school, get good grades, to become a doctor, lawyer, teacher or a nurse so they can make good money and buy nice things. Most parents and adults are not encouraging their children to get educated on how to own their own doctor's office, law firm, educational institution, and business or to develop their own skills for self-reliance. But instead, they encourage them to spend a decade or more in someone else's school of thought, acquiring someone else's skills to make someone else's dreams become reality.

Many people have grown up, taking advice from their financially illiterate parents and are now buried in debt just as their parents. Upon obtaining their High School Diploma or GED (General Education Development), most youth from unfortunate backgrounds turn to their financially illiterate parents or other elders for advice about making money and obtaining wealth. They, then go on living the rest of their lives in the rat race, which I will discuss in the next chapter. Instead of finding a successful mentor or seeking advice from someone who is financially literate or financially stable, they depend on someone who has never done it, who knows nothing about it, for all the wrong answers.

I am one of those individuals who took the advice to further my education in someone else's school of thought and ended up being over $70,000 in student loan debt. I spent five years in college acquiring someone else's skills to foster someone else's economy and civilization, not to foster the civilization and economy of my people. I wasn't taught how to develop my own skills for self-reliance, but skills needed to depend on someone else for survival and for a means of making a living. The miseducation I received from the Euro-American educational system in terms of creating wealth has been ineffective and has placed me in a financial hole. The learning of this miseducation has inspired me to develop my own skills for survival, to become an entrepreneur and to potentially develop a resource center that would be designed to empower self-knowledge and teach skills for self-reliance.

When we attend school, mostly we learn what works best for our instructor, to retain knowledge to help our employer's dreams manifest, not what works best for us to make our own dreams manifest. When we are sitting in class, and our instructor instruct us to read and to take notes on what she's saying or what is posted on the PowerPoint slides, we are reading someone else's thoughts and taking notes from someone else's submitted information. Why is it that we aren't taught how to generate our own thoughts and taught how to develop our own skills in life? That's because they want us to depend on someone else, the elite, as a means of survival.

If I knew what I know now, back in high school, I would have never attended college. I taught myself how to write books and how to write in general. I taught myself how to think and how to create my own resume and writing services business. With books I purchased from eBay and Amazon, I taught myself how to be myself and how to make my own dreams and desires manifest. School didn't.

The Euro-American education system is non-effective when it comes to self-knowledge and wealth attainment, especially for colored people and it's proven.

There was a time when our people of color weren't allowed to read, write or attend schools. Then, there became a time when we were allowed to attend schools but the schools we attended were nowhere as good as the white schools. We had poor instructors and poor resources. When white supremacists allowed us people of color to attend school, they didn't create an Afro-American education system for us to thrive in. They made us attend their schools and learn under their education system. Which mean, we learned what they allowed us to learn. "The Miseducation."

Today, we are experiencing the same trials we experienced back when we weren't allowed to thrive in education. Colored youth who attend public schools in Cleveland, Ohio, don't have the same resources and chances of success as the elite white students in the Berea city school system. An entire graduating class at Berea High School have a greater chance of success than the valedictorian and the top ten graduates at John Adams High School. The same goes for colleges and universities. The predominantly white colleges have a greater chance of success, than Historically Black Colleges and Universities (HBCU). It has been said that, a colored man with a college degree is equivalent to a white man with a high school diploma.

I'm going to share with you my views on college and the entry level job market from the perspective of a young black man born and raised in poverty and communities dominated by violence.

Many of us in poverty dominated communities, and even suburban communities, have applied to many job positions using our high school diploma or GED. Upon doing so, we have found that the professional job market is very difficult to enter with just a high school diploma and/or GED. Many employers/recruiters have skipped over our resumes and letters of interest after seeing that our highest level of education is high school, that we have no related experience and that our ethnicity is African American.

So many of us turn to our parents, teachers, employers, and others to ask, what is it that we have to do in order to secure the positions we want, so that we can be rich/wealthy? They tell us to further our education. Go to college and get a degree. We then respond by saying, how can we afford college? College is expensive. We don't have any money. Our parents, teachers, employers and other elders then suggest, financial aid. The United States Department of Education will provide you with aid that consists of grants, scholarships and/or loans that will cover some, if not all of your tuition. Grants you won't have to pay back and the loans you can pay back after you complete college.

Here you have some parents and others who have never been to college, and those who may be in student loan debt up to the ceiling, encouraging our youth that college is the only way out. Since, many of our young people are inexperienced and haven't been properly taught or shown how money work, they tend to believe what mom and dad and their elders say right off the back.

Many youths in impoverished environments believe college is they only way to having a great paying career and getting out of poverty, unless they have a special talent such as playing sports, acting or singing. "If I graduate from college, I can get the job I want and live comfortably. If I graduate college, I can escape poverty and get my family out as well."

Sold on the idea that a college education and working for someone for the rest of their lives will get us out of poverty and possibly rich, we decide to apply to a college or university of our choice and get accepted. Being that many of us are first generation college students and our parents aren't financially stable enough to cover our college expenses, we are forced to take out another loan, apply for work study or get a part-time job to cover our college expenses and to support ourselves.

Accepting a work-study position or a part-time student position comes with a great sacrifice such as reducing the number of credits/courses you can take each semester, which means staying in college longer than intended. Also, the longer you stay, the more you spend in tuition and college expenses. Tuition increases every year at most institutions.

Our commencement day arrives. We are all excited that we have no more homework, studying, papers, projects, quizzes, or exams. We have met all of the requirements for graduation and are now among hundreds of thousands who will receive a college degree. Upon walking across the stage and receiving an empty diploma holder, we are released into the real world, to compete among one another for employment.

We return back home and re-apply to our desired positions with our college diploma, applications, resumes (highlighting our education, employment history, skills and qualifications) and with a letter of interest. Employers/recruiters then schedule interviews with us, telling us to be on time and to be prepared.

To prepare for our interview, many of us take the time out to sharpen our interview skills. When interview day arrive, we are properly dressed and are on time. Recruiters then call us back to the office and they begin the interview process.

The job description is reviewed by all parties and the recruiter asks us about our related work experience, skills and abilities we bring to the position. After providing the information asked of us, recruiters then tell us, "Thanks for coming in. I'll be in touch." After a week or two has gone by, they either inform us that they have selected someone who is more qualified for the position or that we don't qualify and need more experience in the field.

Many of us graduates become fed up at this point. We become lost, confused, and feel like we have experienced one big lie. We were told we needed a college degree in order to secure our dream position and to get out of poverty. We have the degree and it isn't enough.

We have spent four or more years in an higher educational institution, doing a ton of homework, studying, term papers, projects, quizzes and exams, to be rejected from our desired employers. And in most cases, the homework, papers, and exams had nothing to do with the job itself.

Ever since high school graduation, we thought, if we attended and graduated from college, it would free us from the life of poverty. Instead, attending college put us $60,000 or more in debt. Keeping us in poverty. Our parents, teachers, pastors, and many others had us convinced that a college degree would open doors to a better future.

So far, the only thing we received was a handshake and a pat on the back from the school's president who really said, "thanks for adding to my salary and good luck getting out of debt," and those who have seen us in our cap and gown.

Being that I am a first-generation college graduate and had those experiences personally regarding securing employment, I noticed something.

During most interviews, candidates are asked questions that could have been found on their submitted resumes and letters of interest. Many employers/recruiters do not take the time out to prepare for the interviews they conduct. They do not take the time to fully review their candidates submitted information, which causes the interviewer to waste the candidate's time. If they did review the information submitted, many of the questions asked during the interview wouldn't be asked.

Questions pertaining to the position could be asked and answered over the telephone or webcam to save time. Instead, candidates are forced to waste their time and money on transportation going to these interviews, for questions that could be answered over the telephone or webcam, or by reading the submitted information.

Many candidates with degrees have applied to hundreds of hiring jobs, and have only had a handful of interviews. Most possess sharp interview skills as well as exceptional written and oral communication skills. But good interviewing skills and a college degree is not enough to land the job they desire. Most employers are more interested in candidates who have working experience, rather they have a high school diploma or a college degree or those who have been referred by someone the employer personally know. In some cases, a candidate with working experience who possess a high school diploma is more likely to land the job quicker than someone with no working experience but holds a college degree. Especially if the person with the high school diploma is Caucasian and the person with the college degree is Black/ African American.

I mentioned in my first book, *How Success Became My Focus* that, while browsing Arlene Schwartz Personalized Resume Services website, I realized why employers either looked passed candidates resumes or did not receive them at all. I've learned that at most corporations, no live person actually reads resumes. Instead, they are scanned into the candidate database by the ATS (Advanced Applicant Tracking Systems). Most systems do nothing with the resumes until they are specifically asked by a recruiter or manager to search through them for a specific job opening. Resumes can sit in the database and never be read by a human being. Only if a recruiter or manager decides to search the database after the hundreds of thousands of resumes are electronically narrowed down to a manageable number (usually less than a hundred), is it possible for someone to actually "read" a candidate's resume. Recruiters who do search databases generally do it only one day per week and, if a candidate's resume didn't come in that day, it will probably be lost in the volume of thousands of resumes that will arrive before the next search.

I've also learned that applicant tracking systems sort resumes primarily based on the number of keywords in the resume. If candidates fail to use the right keywords, there is no chance their resume will be read by a human being.

You must also know that the use of wrong keywords isn't the only disqualifying factor for not landing a job. Your name, gender, age, religion, race/ethnicity, and political views could also be grounds for disqualification, regardless if you have a degree or experience. Many corporations are bound by their state to not discriminate against, gender, age, or other character traits, but they do anyway. They will use an excuse such as, you don't meet the requirements, or we have selected a more qualified candidate, or any other excuse they come up with to hide their true reason for disqualifying you.

If you are Black/African American or Hispanic, you may have been victimized many times. Many years invested in education, job training and hours of interview preparation, to be denied the position you are qualified for because you are Black/African-American or Hispanic as opposed to your inability to do the job.

Brothers and sisters, my job isn't to deter you from going to college because getting an education at a college is important in terms of gaining general knowledge and preparing for the working field. It's also a great source for networking.

However, if you are using college as a tool to acquire wealth, you are wasting your time. Schools aren't designed to produce employers, instead they are designed to produce good employees. Warren Bennis said, "universities, unfortunately are not always the best place to learn… They are producing throngs of narrow-minded specialist who may be wizards at making money, but who are unfinished as people. These specialists have been taught how to do, but they have not learned how to be." Many colleges educated individuals are very grateful of their academic credentials and have forgotten that most successful individuals and the individuals who have shaped this country didn't have MBAs and PhDs.

I would like to become financially wealthy someday. I do not wish to be a servant of someone else's business for the rest of my life, where I have no control and where my people aren't benefiting from their labor. If you enjoy working for someone and want to climb the corporate ladder, go to college. To me college wasn't worth getting $70,000 in debt to compete for employment and to have no control of the business I'm accepted in.

Those of you who are in college and those who are thinking about attending college, make sure that you are doing it for you and not for anyone else. Make sure it's what you are passionate about. I say this because, there are many people who have wasted years and years chasing someone else's dreams, desires and success. Many of them, now realize that what they are doing isn't all that great. In fact, they hate it. They are now stuck and don't have the time, money or patience to start over.

A study by the Carnegie Foundation shows that an increasing number of young people choose fields that promise to be instant profitable such as computer science, healthcare programs, engineering and business. These fields have been chosen mainly because a parent or teacher encouraged it by saying, "it pays well," not because they enjoy the industry where they will work. Today, very few people have an academic background that matches in anyway what they are doing.

For instance, I have a Bachelor of Arts Degree in Criminology and Justice Studies from Kent State University and I don't do criminal justice work. I work in Corrections, which is close to it, but it's not what my degree trained me to do. I have authored two books (working on books 3 and 4), I coach people during times of change and empathize with their perspectives. I'm an inspirational writer. I revamp resumes and cover letters. I write poetry, take and edit pictures/videos, cook, conduct speaking engagements and do a host of other things. I have no academic credentials for any of them. Most individuals I meet believe I majored in journalism, business, or liberal arts. They would never guess criminal justice. I enjoy being the leader that I am. A college degree did not make me into the person I am today. My self-actualization did.

Many of America's most talented and successful people had a liberal arts background, including over forty percent of all CEO's.

A liberal arts education is probably the best form of education for an entertainment business. American television executive, Barbara Corday said, she feels she has a liberal arts degree even though she doesn't have a degree to show it. She goes on and say a lot of young people have all sorts of degrees, but they lack some of the personality traits like showmanship and enthusiasm and childlike qualities that the entertainment business requires. People who go to plays, read books, know the classics, who have an open mind, and enjoy experiences are more apt to be successful in the entertainment business than someone with an MBA in finance.

As I mentioned earlier, many of the most successful people and those who have shaped this country didn't have MBAs and PhDs or any other college degree.

The primary lesson I learned at Salem International University and Kent State University, and what many other successful individuals around the world have learned, was we didn't need to go to school to become successful. Renn Zaphiropoulos, founder of Versatec, said education began at home. He was brought up by Greek parents in Egypt. He mentioned that his father was a sea captain and didn't have college degrees, but he had been everywhere and was a heavy reader. Zaphiropoulos father told him that, 'Your house is your university.' Instead, of going to church, they listened to classical music on Sundays. His father was a poet. His advice to his son was, "never do anything because other people do it, but because it makes good sense to you."

Zaphiropoulos was a good student but not a straight A student. He said, straight "A" students never seem to get over it. He had other interests such as painting, composing and writing poems. He goes on and say, "It's easy enough to learn marketing, selling, engineering, or whatever. It's harder to learn how to optimize your own performance and that of your subordinates."

You do not need a degree to become yourself and to live out your purpose. My degree is just a frame on the wall., I hardly ever look at it. College taught me "perseverance." I learned enough to know that I can do anything I put my mind to. Majority of the wisdom and knowledge I possess have been self-taught.

It's important that we understand the meaning of having a true education. A true education won't allow us to develop other people's skills, rather skills of our own. It will empower us to obtain self-knowledge for self-determination and self-reliance. Each and everyone of us was created differently and we all have a different purpose in life. No one was created the same. Therefore, we must not limit our image, education and success to social standards. We must limit our image, education and success to our own liking and be proud to have ownership of what we possess.

We are now living in the information age, which means whatever information we need to accomplish our desired goals is out here. You don't have to go to college if you don't want to. We now have the internet, public libraries, university libraries, successful mentors, seminars etc. that will educate us on becoming what and who we want to become. There is so much information out here today we can teach ourselves how to build our own empire. Using the resources that are available today, such as the internet, libraries, and seminars, you can save thousands of dollars and a ton of time using those resources instead of spending four years or more in a university that teaches you nothing about obtaining wealth or becoming yourself. It was the industrial age when we were taught that, working for someone else's business for thirty years is the American Dream, and that their businesses will pay for life after retirement. We are no longer in the industrial age. We are in the information age.

"Some people come into this world knowing who they want to become, what they want to do, and even how to do it. The rest of us do not have it so easily. We spend a great amount of time deciding what it is we want to be and what we want to do with our lives," says Warren Bennis.

He says, "vague goals such as, 'I just want to be happy' or 'I want to live well' or 'I want to make the world a better place' or even 'I want to be very, very rich' are nearly useless." But so are overly specific goals such as, 'I want to be chairperson of the Microsoft Corporation' or 'I want to find the cure for AIDS.' It's important not to have any specific ambitions or desires.

"It's important to have ambitions in terms of the way you want to live your life and then other things will flow out of that" says, Jamie Raskin, constitutional law and legislation professor at American University and at Washington College of Law.

Schools are designed to produce good employees instead of employers. Employees who benefit the elite and their lives, not the lives of the poor and middle class. You should work toward becoming your own employer, so you can live the life that you desire while benefiting the people in need as opposed to living the life your boss chooses for you.

The next chapter is dedicated to those who are tired of competing in the crowded job market and who want to get out of the rat-race. You will learn that an employee with a safe, secure job without financial aptitude has no escape.

"It's not about how much money you make. It's how much money you keep. If you work for money, you give the power up to your employer. If your money work for you, you keep and control the power. The only report card that matters is your income statement (financial statement)."

— *JAMEEL DAVIS*

Chapter Three

AVOID THE RAT RACE & RETIRE YOUNG

"If you are going to spend the rest of your life borrowing other people's money, make sure you are given enough leverage to get you on the road to financial freedom"

— JAMEEL DAVIS

During grade school, our main concern were the grades we received on our report cards. Our parents would arrive to our schools on report card pick up day and we would hope and pray that our teacher gave us excellent grades so our parents wouldn't be upset or wouldn't punish us. After many years of grade school and college, I found the only report card that truly matters is your financial statement.

"Early in life, most people are programmed to mind other people's businesses and to make other people rich" says, Robert Kiyosaki, in his book *Cash Flow Quadrant.* He says it begins with words of advice such as these:

1. Go to school and get good grades, so you can find a safe, secure job with good pay and benefits.
2. Work hard so you can buy the house of your dreams. After all, your home is an asset and it is your most important investment. Having a large mortgage is good because the government gives you a tax deduction for your interest payments.
3. "Buy Now, Pay Later" or "Low Down, easy monthly payments." Or "Come in and save money."

People who blindly follow these words of advice often become: employees who make their bosses and owners richer, debtors who make banks and money lenders rich, taxpayers who make the government rich and consumers who make many other businesses rich.

Instead of finding their own financial fast track, they help everyone else find theirs. Instead of minding their own business, they work all their lives minding everyone else's.

I was often asked at my places of employment, "Why don't you do overtime?" and I often replied, "Because I don't need it. I live within my means and besides it's unhealthy."

Many people who do volunteer overtime at their place of employment have huge balloon payments to make: mortgage payments, property taxes, auto loans, credit card payments, boat loans, cable television etc. They also have to make up for their large unnecessary spending on expensive tennis shoes, dinner tabs, outfits, jewelry, hair and hair products, cosmetics, custom tires, rims, paint jobs, bottle service at nightclubs etc.

That unnecessary spending is the reason the poor is poor and the rich is rich. Not because the rich pay less in taxes. I will discuss taxes later in the chapter. The rich create items and businesses such as those mentioned above, for us to spend our money on and businesses for us to spend our money in. They design and cover the marketing for their products and businesses, so we can continue to spend our money carelessly (making them richer), trying to fit in, and by trying to impress others.

In poverty dominated communities like Cleveland, Ohio, Arabs and Middle Easterners own the corner stores, hair stores and gas stations. Their stores and gas stations cater to the wants, needs, and to the destruction of the people they serve. They don't just sell gas and groceries at their stores. They sell tobacco, alcohol, lottery tickets, junk food, cell phones etc. The products and services they provide to the community makes them multi-millionaires and many of the people in those communities aren't even aware of it. Many of the store clerks/owners know everyone in the community, but do nothing to better that community. Violence, drugs, and crime is high in the areas they are stationed. Schools look like abandoned property, streets have potholes and properties are destroyed. Their gold mine is in the poor, black community. Where is the gold mine for the poor? Heaven, when we die?

Every dollar we spend determines how poorer we will be and how richer someone else will become.

Majority of the poor and middle class are busy living like they are rich, not knowing how the rich live. They make assumptions based off what they hear in music and what they see on the television screen. They hear their favorite artist sing or rap about material possessions, such as Rolex watches, Red Bottoms, Louis Vuitton bags, Jordans etc., then run and spend their hard-earned money on the items mentioned in the songs, saying, "If Chris Brown is wearing Jordans, I have to get Jordans."

Many see their favorite movie star with foreign objects and either spend their entire paycheck, withdraw their savings, or take someone else's money or material possessions to buy the items seen on television.

While many of the poor and middle class is attempting to live rich, spending all of their hard-earned money on nice things, living flashy and putting everything in their name, the rich is living like they are poor, investing their money, and keeping it in circulation. They are getting everything out of their name and living a non-flashy lifestyle. The ones you see who are flashy are the ones who are getting paid to be flashy, so they can trap you into buying the flashy things they possess. Their job is to get you to buy it in order to make the manufacturers and owners richer, so they can get paid from them. It's called social engineering and population control.

Although there is nothing really wrong with spending your own money, but how many people have planned for the long run; short term, mid-term, long term, health care, education, retirement, and leaving money back for their family once they have left Earth?

Jordan shoes and Nike Lebrons are liabilities if your asset column isn't purchasing them for you. Jordan shoes and Nike Lebrons are assets to Michael Jordan and Lebron James. When you purchase them with your hard-earned money, you make them richer and make yourself poorer.

What is your business? Who's paying you for your products and services? If you do not have a business and don't have anyone purchasing products and services from you, what business can you create so people can pay you for your products and services?

The reason the rich don't put all their valuables in their name and why many don't live flashy is because it can be easily taken away from them. If someone sue you in civil court and win and you don't have cash to pay, they are coming after your valuables and assets: properties, businesses, stocks and bonds of equal value. Many don't live flashy for fear that someone from a less fortunate background may rob or even kill them for something as small as an iPhone.

Though the rich may have some nice possessions, their assets paid for them. They didn't have to work hard for someone else to acquire their items. Many of us, he poor and middle class, work hard for someone else to acquire liabilities we think are assets such as a car, boat, and the home we are living in.

The rich work smart and hard for themselves to obtain their assets. They create businesses people need, then hire the poor and middle-class people to run their businesses. Their businesses pay for the items they desire: their dream home, private jets and vacation resorts. We, the poor and middle class, create excuses as to why we don't have any money and blame everyone else but ourselves for our lack. We say, "I had to pay bills" or "I loaned it to a friend" or "I spent it all on my car payment, hair, food, transportation" or "They wouldn't hire me."

We are hired by the wealthy and rely on our employers to pay for our retirement after working for them for nearly thirty years.

Speaking of retirement. It's harmful and selfish of us to work thirty or more years making someone else rich. How many people you know have become wealthy after retiring from working thirty years? Maybe none. How many people you know have sustained major health problems or have died during or after their period of working? Maybe many.

Working to make the rich richer and to make ourselves poorer is very, very selfish. It is selfish not only to ourselves but to our family.

We spend our entire life minding someone else's business instead of minding our own. We speed to work every morning trying to beat traffic to punch someone's clock for eight or more hours. We are making sure their normal operations is running smoothly, while they are on a beach in their vacation home or relaxing with their family and rich friends. We take time from our family to mind their business, get paid a small amount bi-weekly to cover housing costs, food, transportation, and small entertainment while they get paid millions of dollars off our hard labor. Our hard labor pays for their vacation in Bora Bora and to live in multi-million-dollar mansions.

It's also selfish of us to take our hard-earned money we obtain from our billion-dollar employers and spend it in other businesses without paying ourselves first. What I mean by that is receiving our paycheck then spending it all on bills and items we don't necessarily need, leaving us flat broke before the next pay period.

To pay yourself first means to mind your business first, taking care of you before minding someone else's business.

When you receive your paycheck, before paying a bill, giving it away and spending it on wants and needs, take out how much you think you deserve after that 40-hour work week and put it to the side (in a short term, midterm and long-term savings account). You should pay yourself at least 20 percent of your monthly income: 5 percent for short term, 5 percent for midterm and 10 percent for long term. If your job has 401K, at least 10-15 percent of your pay should already be going into your long-term account. If you already have a 401K plan, you can add the additional 10 percent to your short and midterm accounts.

Next, pay your bills and purchase your necessities. If there is anything left over, buy what you want. What's left over from that, put back in your savings. If you fall short of covering an expense, think of ways to create money to cover that expense before touching your savings. If all ideas fail and the expense is a necessity, use your savings and put the leftover change from that expense back into your savings. Do this every pay.

Once your account becomes healthy, begin taking a portion of your income and put it into and investment savings account so you can fund your own business, rather it be a rental property or storefront. For every balloon payment you receive, rather it be a large paycheck, insurance claim or the lottery, be sure to pay yourself first. Everyone else get paid, so why can't you? Work smart, not hard. That's what the rich do.

You should also begin building your raining day, emergency (911) account. It's important to have a 911 account so you won't have to scramble looking for money to cover any unexpected expenses. If you are starting out, $1000 should be your goal to have saved in your 911 account. Once your goal is reached, continue to add to it. Try to have at least three to six months of monthly expenses saved in your 911 account. Therefore, if you lose your job, you will have enough money saved where you don't have to panic about covering housing payments, buying food and clothes.

Three to six months is the average time frame for someone to secure new employment. If your monthly expenses total $1200, at three months of saving you should have $3600 in your 911 account. At six months of savings, you should have $7200. I encourage couples to have separate 911 accounts, as well as a joint 911 account. A joint emergency fund is for emergencies that involve the entire household. When a joint 911 account is decided, keep track of how much money is deposited by each of you so there won't be any confusions. Your separate account is for personal emergency purposes such as if things go south with you and your partner and one of you decide to leave the home for good. You don't want to have to panic or scramble to find money or risk sleeping on the street. You will have money for a hotel room for a few nights, just until you find you a place to live. You will also have money for an investment of your choice.

People who have their finances in order are, in some cases, the happiest. Their family is happy and the people around them are happy.

People who do not have their finances in order are, in some cases, the most unhappiest and miserable. They are jealous, envious, in an unhappy relationship, and are often depressed and angry. Many commit crimes of theft, fraud, robbery, and burglary. Healthy finances help boost self-esteem.

When I first started working at the sheriff's department in Cleveland back in September 2013, in the Corrections Division, I was informed of a gentleman who made well over $100,000 in a year as a corrections officer. My first thought, "He's going to work himself to death." The idea of going to school, getting good grades, graduating from college, securing a decent job and retiring, didn't matter much to me once I was hired in as a corrections officer.

After I heard about the gentleman who made over 100 grands, I assumed he had to be at least 35 years old, 11 years older than me at the time.

After about a week of being employed, I met the gentleman and he appeared to be around 70 years of age. From that moment on, I knew working thirty years for someone would not give me financial freedom. My colleague, who is three times my age, is punching the same clock as I, but punching it way more rapidly just to make over $100,000. I saw something wrong with that picture. That would be me in 30 years if I stayed put as an employee.

I believe someone at the age of 70 should be happily retired from labor duties: residing on a beachfront, spending the rest of their living days with their family, while watching their money grow for the generations that come after them.

That moment when I met him, I told myself I would not live that way. I began creating and executing my plan to financial freedom using the money I obtain from my employer.

The hundred grand a year guy has set the bar for other corrections officers at the county jail. Many officers have tried to accomplish that goal or exceed it. Many have gotten close. They are working hard to make a little money for the purpose of spending it all in someone else's establishment.

If you are going to mind someone else's business, save some energy for yours. Don't die helping someone else's business succeed without helping yours or your family.

Someone once said, "Spending four years working on a business is risky." Someone else replied, "No, spending 30 years working for someone is risky."

Individuals who work for an extensive period of time are at extreme risk for major health problems, especially, the ones who do a lot of overtime. Your body need adequate rest, food and exercise so it can perform well. When you prevent your body from receiving the rest, food and exercise it need, your body's systems begin to break down, making it harder and harder to fight off infections, diseases, and to heal injuries. Years and years of wear and tear from overworking yourself, shortens your lifespan and makes it harder to partake in activities and events you enjoy.

Let us cut back on the heavy spending. Let's save, invest, create business opportunities, obtain short term and long-term care insurance, eat good, exercise and retire healthy. Don't wait until the last minute. It will be too late.

One thing I suggest you do right away is get a life insurance policy. Life insurance policies cover your death expenses, your leftover debt, and will leave money back to your family depending on how much coverage you purchase and how much debt you are responsible for paying. You don't want your family to be stuck with your debt when you leave this Earth. Their grieving plus your debt and theirs will cause more pain. Get your life insurance policy now.

There are three types of people in the world: 1.) the ones who create the money 2.) the ones who work for the money 3.) and those who do not have any.

Only 10 percent of the people in the world have the wealth, while the other 90 percent do not. Some babies are/were born into wealth, while some are and were born into the middle class, and the majority born into poverty. If you are like me, person 2 and 3, working for those who create the money and born into poverty, then you know that, wealth is not taught in our homes nor in our schools. In fact, we know that, majority of the colleges and universities don't teach it either.

Our grandparents, their parents and so forth, were taught to go to school and to get an education, so they can obtain a high paying job to buy nice things. They were not taught how to create money or how to have money work for them. Instead, they were taught how to work for it and how to make their employers wealthier. That same system that was embedded in their minds, have been passed down generation after generation. Instead, of being taught how to explore our six sense, which is "creative imagination," or to make our own imagination of wealth become a reality, we're taught how to make someone else's imagination become reality.

It's time we use our creative imagination again. The one we had when we were a child. Let's start dreaming again and start making our dreams become reality. As I mentioned in Chapter 2, we are now living in the information age, which means, whatever information we need to accomplish our desired dreams and goals, it's out here. Especially since we have advanced technology such as computers, tablets, and the internet. We have access to public libraries, university libraries, research labs, successful mentors etc.

The Industrial Age sold the average American on the idea of getting a "good job" that would allow you to buy a home, a car, take care of your family and retire after 30 years of working at least 40 hours a week. It left many, for generations to come, believing these "big" businesses will pay for your life after retirement. Now, that we are in the information age, we can create our dream business and it can pay for the life we desire.

What are you doing with your income once you receive it? The IRS (Internal Revenue Service) asks this question when they view your taxes every year. When the IRS reviews your financial statement, they look and see if you have purchased any assets, items and services for your assets, gave donations or if you spent majority of your income on liabilities.

If you purchase assets, items, and services for your assets, or give donations, most of those expenses will be deducted from your taxes, which will result in a larger tax return (refund) for you. If majority of your money is spent on services you do not need, and you don't have any assets to maintain or any dependents, you will receive a much smaller tax return.

There has been a myth circulating America for decades stating that, the rich are rich because they don't pay taxes. The fact of the matter is, the rich do pay taxes. They just don't pay as much as the poor and middle class. As I mentioned previously, if you purchase assets and items to maintain them or give donations, those expenses can be deducted from the amount you owe in taxes.

Since the rich own assets, they spend first and get taxed later. The poor and the middle class get taxed before and after they spend. You receive tax breaks if you own a business. If your financial statements, your lifetime report card don't have any A's (assets) on them, it's going to be difficult passing on to the next class (from poor to middle and from middle to rich). If you are in the poor and middle class, you will have to learn and understand financial literacy and taxes if you want to advance to the upper class. Those two subjects will get you on the road to financial freedom.

What is financial literacy? Financial literacy is the ability to understand how money works in the world: how someone earns it, how that person manages it, how he/she invests it (turn it into more), and how that person donates it to help others.

What are taxes? Taxes are compulsory contributions to state revenue, levied by the government on workers' income and business profits or added to the cost of some goods, services, and transactions. How does taxes work? **Elizabeth Rosen** will help you understand below.

The money collected from **taxes** goes towards federal education programs, the U.S. military, welfare programs, and various agencies (such as the EPA and FDA). Both individuals and companies are required to remit a portion of their income to the federal government on an annual basis. If/ when politicians decide that more money is needed for certain programs, they often raise taxes to pay for them.

While legislators construct and implement tax laws, the IRS is the federal agency in charge of enforcing those tax laws and collecting the taxes.

The amount of tax that you owe each year is based on your income level. The United States currently uses a progressive income tax system — which means that the more money you earn, the more taxes you have to pay. Fortunately, there are ways you can reduce your income tax liability by using various **tax credits, tax deductions,** tax exclusions, and other tax breaks.

The majority of individuals are subject to the "Pay-As-You-Go" system, which means that their income tax is deducted from each paycheck and sent to the IRS. This is also referred to as **withholding tax.** If you are **self-employed,** the IRS expects you to pay income tax on a quarterly basis (typically in equal installments every three months).

At the end of the year, if your payments were not enough to cover the total income tax due, you must pay the rest to the IRS. Conversely, if you paid too much over the course of the year (more than what you owe in income tax), the IRS will send back your excess payment in the form of a **tax refund.**

You need financial literacy in order to live out the life of your dreams. Understanding taxes will help you receive larger tax returns and will help you get tax breaks once your asset column is established. Before learning taxes, you must first know which assets don't carry a tax shelter.

However, just because an asset doesn't carry a tax shelter, doesn't mean it will not produce cash flow. See *Rich Dad's Guide To Investing* by Robert Kiyosaki to learn more about the different types of investment opportunities and their tax shelter.

Although having huge tax breaks is great, it shouldn't be the main reason why you invest in such assets. You must love your investments.

I know that you would want your assets to be both powerful and stable and to provide cash flow. An asset that is powerful has protection. It has a tax shelter and is protected by a corporation (a company or group of people authorized to act as a single entity (legally a person) and recognized as such in law).

A stable asset rarely fluctuates. Its market doesn't rise and fall often. An asset that produces cash flow is an asset that pours money into your pocket. Real Estate (property consisting of land or buildings) is a powerful and stable asset that produces cash flow. Stocks (a share in the ownership of a company) and bonds (a debt security, similar to an IOU) provide cash flow and are powerful. However, they are unstable and don't have much protection.

Stocks and bonds are unstable because you can't predict how much money you are going to get out of them. The stock market rises and fall often. So, you must know when to put your money in and when to pull your money out. You may buy and succeed or you may buy and fail.

It's very important that you understand the stock market and any other investments before pouring all of your money into it. You may also want to begin studying financial statements of other businesses so you can determine if their business is worth investing in.

A financial statement will show you the strengths and weaknesses of that business, kind of like the progress reports you received in grade school. Don't be a fool pouring all your money into a very weak investment.

Real estate, on the other hand, is stable and powerful. It produces cash flow. Real estate might not produce cash flow as quickly as stocks but, with time and the right investment properties, cash will be flowing into your account every month.

Real estate is stable because the market doesn't rise and fall often. Therefore, you are able to calculate your earning potential. Also, as long as babies are being born, there will always be a high demand for residential property. People are always going to need a place to live. Real estate is protected by insurance houses, corporations, and have huge tax shelters. It also produces cash flow.

Rare coins, gold and silver are other powerful, stable and cash flow producing assets. Financial experts have said, after each investment you purchase, purchase an ounce of gold and silver. Gold and silver will increase in value over time. In case your investments fail, you can cash in your hard assets (gold and silver) and start again.

Many people think that diversifying assets is very risky. There is nothing wrong with diversifying your assets because, in order to have financial freedom, you need cash flowing in from as many pipelines as possible.

However, before diversifying your assets, it's important that you master one before going on to the next. You don't want to get crushed in someone else's game. Protect yourself by learning and understanding your investments.

If real estate, stocks and bonds, rare coins or gold and silver, do not have your interest, launch your own business, to get you on the road to financial freedom. If you choose to create your own establishment, you can hire your own business managers that will maintain the daily operations of your business, allowing you to do the things you enjoy.

My financial plan focuses on using the least amount of time to make the greatest amount of money, using the least amount of effort so I can spend more time doing the things I enjoy and with those who matter the most.

Watching the stock market 24/7 is too time consuming for me and it would require a lot of effort to maintain. Real estate requires a lot of attention in the beginning but, after a while, it doesn't have to be monitored often. Especially if your properties are under a property management company.

Working forty years, investing a ton of time and effort into someone else's establishment is unfair to me, my health and my family. I would never have time to mind my own business and I will miss out on valuable time with my loved ones and doing things I enjoy most.

The idea for many is to have money work for them so they can live the life they desire. When you work for money, you lose that opportunity and you leave that power in your boss's hands.

Your boss will make the decision to approve or disapprove your time off requests. By becoming your own boss, you can make those decisions yourself. Your boss will penalize you for being tardy or absent, because it disrupts the normal operations of his business. Take control of your life and your money by hiring yourself. Approve your own time off requests and vacation time.

There are many people who enjoy working for others and who don't want to have their own money. They enjoy being controlled by their bosses. If owning a business is not what you want, but you are content with working for someone until retirement and want to advance in the company, your next position may not be advertised. Daniel Bartz, writer of the article, *Your Next Job Probably Won't Be Advertised*, suggests you do the following:

Talk to top recruiters:

Higher up, human resources representatives tend to be gatekeepers for higher-level positions. Identify recruiters with sway at the businesses you admire.

Make a friend on the inside:

It can pay to establish relationships with peers at companies on your wishlist. Use LinkedIn to find a second-degree connection, then request an introduction from your mutual pal. Don't say, "can you help me get a job" or the person will feel used. Offer something in return like an introduction to influences in your network.

Get your boss's buy-in:

Tell your boss, "Under your direction, I've learned so much and feel ready to take on a higher role. Can you help me find new opportunities here?" If that is uncomfortable, schedule a visit with the head of Human Resources. Tell that person you're interested in moving up, and why.

While on your journey to financial freedom, unless you are content where you are right now, you have to be a little stingy in terms of money. I'm not saying, don't give back to those in need. I'm saying don't give back to those who have been around but have refused to help you achieve your dreams and desired goals. It's unfair to you and your family to give up your hard-earned royalties to those who have the easiest job of sticking their hand out and asking for your money.

Those who haven't offered a single hand of support and those who have been around and watched you day in and day out work your butt off to receive your royalties, should be given a firm "NO" when they ask for your money to cover their expenses. It's important that you remove such people from your surroundings if possible. Even family members. You don't see financial institutions lending out free money without running a credit check, background check and without charging interest. So, why should you?

If you find it difficult telling people "no" when they ask for your money, try treating them as if they were your employee. Have them work for it. If they want to borrow your money, treat them as if they were a customer at a financial institution taking out a loan. Enter into a contract or agreement and charge interest. This helps keep you from being used and helps make them a loyal employee or borrower, especially if you pay good. Better yet, it may keep them from asking.

You would be better off giving donations to charity foundations and to those who truly are in need because you will be supporting a good cause and your donations can be deducted from what you owe in taxes at tax time. Giving to couch potatoes won't save you money at tax time and it will only make them more and more lazy. If you continue to hand them money, they will never get off the couch and go get their own. Why would they, if all they have to do is ask you? Invest in yourself first, before investing in and supporting someone who do not support you.

"Intelligence solves problems and produces money. Money without financial intelligence, is money soon gone."

— *ROBERT KIYOSAKI*

"Many people make excuses for why they live a certain way:

My parents didn't have any money' or 'the government doesn't help us,' or 'the rich have all the money and they don't pay taxes.'

If your parents didn't have it to give to you and the government isn't helping you, that means you have to go get it yourself.

Once you reach a certain age in life, you can no longer make excuses and blame others for your lack and unhappy life.

Stop sitting around waiting for someone to hand it to you because they aren't coming.

Think outside the box, get out your comfort zone and go get it."

— *JAMEEL DAVIS*

Money is measured in quantity, by numbers. Numbers are infinity.

If numbers are infinite, so is money. So why chase money if you can never have it all?

Don't waste life worrying about how much money you do not have. Living is free.

Spend life having fun and creating memorable experiences.

— *JAMEEL DAVIS*

Chapter Four

I AM MY BROTHERS & SISTERS' KEEPER

"All life was interrelated, all humanity part of one process, and to the degree that I harm my brother, to that extent I am harming myself"

— MARTIN LUTHER KING JR

I like to think of myself as an, educator, philosopher, and/or life coach, even though I do not have the academic credentials for those titles. Society require you to obtain those credentials from an accredited college or university, in order to practice, and/or to work for a business or corporation. However, I do not operate within society's standards and my life experiences are the best teachers of all. That's how I was able to produce this book.

I took it upon myself to become educated on the things that are of an importance to me and to my survival. I also took it upon myself to think on my own and to learn how to educate others. I have connected with my infinite spirit, which has given me direction and wisdom.

A man's purpose in life is to lead, build, educate, protect, provide, and to serve his family as well as his community. I am living in my purpose.

It is my passion to enlighten and to help myself, as well as those who wish to be helped, to become better than yesterday. I have impacted the lives of many; young and old, male and female, in positive ways. I've educated them in the areas of self-identity, self-discipline, self-determination, respect, relationships, and in many other areas of life. I

49

have also made an impact by leading by example, keeping my word and being the change, I wanted to see in myself, in others and in society. I have eliminated hatred, envy, jealousy, selfishness, and self-doubt from my subconscious mind. I have developed love for all humanity because I know that a negative attitude toward others will never bring me true success.

I rather create friendships and relationships with those who have done the same and who are working towards those changes.

Eliminating negative tendencies from my subconscious mind resulted in me being the successful, educated and highly respected individual that I am today. I see the best in others because I can see the best in me. When they see the best in me, I achieve all that I can be.

Unfortunately, too many blacks fail to see themselves in this light and oppression has played a major part.

Looking at oppression from a high level, as well as the dehumanization of African people, in order for the dominant American society to have risen and to have achieved as much as they have now, they had to destroy the leadership and the minds of our African families. They did so by removing the masculine male from the equation. He was the leader, builder, educator, protector, provider, for his family and community. They used the "divide and conquer" method.

One way they made our African men weak was by brutalizing their children and raping their wives. African males were shackled, forced to witness the abuse, unable to protect their loved ones. They also made our families weak by auctioning off husbands, wives and children to different slave owners who had different plantations located far away. We were deprived of our history, religion, origin, and connections to our families, causing us to not know thyself and to self-destruct. This is what made us weak.

Removing African men from the home made it easier for them to reprogram, rape, and capture our women and our children.

Looking at society today, circumstances are created which deprive us African-Americans of our origin, purpose, and connections to our families which causes us to not know thyself. There are little to no traces of our ancestors.

History books, television shows, music and images do not reveal true African history, excellence, or purpose.

Black men are still auctioned off, now into the prison systems designed to drain our energy, break us mentally and to destroy our families. Black men are being auctioned off into cemeteries by justifiable homicides at the hands of uniformed officers and white supremacists.

With our men being removed from the home by either incarceration, death, or by the lack of being a father, our children and their mother are left at home as victims to the government, victims to rapists, victims to robbers, victims to burglars and victims to other violence.

We aren't there to protect them because our life ends as a result of violence in our communities or rogue police officers, because we are incarcerated and because we have been influenced that not raising a family is cool.

Our women and children are auctioned off into the welfare system which is programming them to be content with lack, not having a male presence in the home and to become depended on the government for survival. Not us Black men. A system created by white supremacy.

With the leadership destroyed in our families and with us being separated from our families, our women and children are also conditioned to turn to those poisoned television shows, music, movies and social media as a means of education and direction.

As a result of the conditioning and deprogramming of our men, many single mothers and women are searching for the love and protection they desire through social media. They are spending multiple hours a day surfing the internet, hitting the like button on Facebook and commenting on pictures of men they are physically attracted to on Instagram. They are chasing unfit men all while their children are being neglected.

Their child(ren) begin getting poor reports from school, falling behind in school, dropping out of school, hanging with troubled youth, joining gangs, selling drugs, abusing drugs, shooting, killing, posting half naked pictures on social media for 100 + likes and comments, and seeking the attention from strangers, the kind they did not receive from mom and dad.

Our parents lack of education and knowledge caused by our oppressors, our abandonment, our incarceration, our lost of life to the streets, the neglect of our children by chasing love in all the wrong places, and by not finding our children positive mentors have caused our child(ren) to develop that kind of lifestyle. Parents, we no longer have to wonder why our baby girl or baby boy, may have chosen a different path in life.

Our lack in the above areas and what I will mention below may have resulted in our baby boy or baby girl growing up without proper direction, tracing our footsteps, being abused, thrown in jail and turning to the streets for love, money, and attention.

The poisoned television, music, films and images - which are controlled by the government and our oppressors - are destroying the minds of African Americans by conditioning us to live our lives based upon what we are forced to observe. This prevents us from living out our true purpose. These circumstances are the cause of our men, women and children becoming mentally weak, a "SLAVE (Severely Limited at Valuing Education) to this system of corruption in America.

The social engineering from poisoned television, music, films, and images, forces our young and older people to lose their life to the streets or to incarceration, just as many others have already done. Many of our young sisters who observe the sex scenes on television, film and on social media are conditioned to begin seeking sex around the age of twelve, resulting in them birthing kids at fourteen, searching for the love of a man and a father for their child(ren), just as their mother had done.

Slave owners wanted young black girls to produce children as early as possible, so the owners could capitalize off their births. The fathers of their children would then disappear (rather sold, killed, or escaped to freedom) and the young girls would risk searching for the love of her father or the love of a man for her and her child. Does this ring a bell in society today?

As we already know, media has a huge influence on one's life. Many Black professionals in those industries, that take on the negative roles, may be doing it for a paycheck and not think twice about how their actions and roles impact the many people that are observing.

However, there are some who are taking on these roles to discourage you from doing something positive in your life. Many people, especially young people, tend to take what they observe on television, film and radio, and incorporate it into their personal lives. Many begin purchasing alcohol, drugs, guns, other weapons and items to live the life of those seen on television or those whom they have heard over the radio.

In reading Dr. Maulana Karenga's article, *Beyond Minstrels, Mammy, and Mascots: Demanding and Practicing Respect,* he reminds us to remember Amilcar Cabral's teaching that, regardless of the problems imposed by our oppressor, the greatest struggle we wage is the struggle to overcome ourselves. Dr. Karenga goes on and say, "We must struggle against dancing in our own degradation, buying and listening to music and watching movies and television shows that mangle us and denies us respect around the world. We have to prevent collaborating in our own oppression. We must stand up against those who delight in and distribute our oppressor's racist and degrading doctrines."

He says it's highly imperative that we have a new approach and understanding to our talents and arts. Not only must we judge our arts for its creativity but also for its respect and social relevance for its subject, especially when our people are the subject. Artists who have no respect for their subject can only degrade and distort it and thus collaborate in the projects of our oppressor. One of the greatest challenges facing us as a people is the established order's attempt to use our art to degrade, indict and dismiss us through its distorted projections in the media as well as the established order's cultivation of the conditions, psychology of compulsive racial self-exposure and self-degradation, and its reintroduction of the minstrel, mammy and mascot as fundamental modes of Black self-presentation and self-understanding. Dr. Karenga describes the role of a minstrel, mammy and mascot below:

The minstrel is best described as the gangsta rapper and the self-degrading comedian who are defined by lack of boundaries of decency and dignity. Unlike minstrels of the past, they are not socially forced to perform these self-disfiguring tricks. On the opposite, they delight in it and in attacking the community, other people of color, women, the disabled, the aged, and other marginalized and vulnerable groups.

The mammy is the O'Haras' outspoken housemaid in "Gone with The Wind," who is constantly looking for an opportunity to feed and support the White man, woman and child. Whether it's a commercial, a movie or TV program, the self-degradation and the degradation of others whether Black Woman or Black Man is done with ease and unreasonable enjoyment as a way to please the paymaster and oppressor. These mammies have no real concern for their children or men; they live for and thru service to the oppressor. There are also male mammies, Black genies and infantilized (treat someone as a child or in a way that denies their maturity in age or experience) giants caring for or playing with little white boys, redoing Bojangles and Shirley Temple roles without the skill or coerced nature of it, or knowledge of its ultimate meaning to them or us.

The mascot is best described as the horde of deformed images that exist only to make the white people look good and to draw a clear distinction between one species of human being (inferior) and another (the superior). They are essentially created to degrade and mock, are always mentally, morally, or physically deficient and in need of white assistance. Inherent in the practice of constructing these images is the need to undermine strong images of Black Men, with roles of melodramatic drag queens, fake radicals (revolutionists) who concede the rightness of the white hero or heroine (a woman admired or idealized for her courage, outstanding achievements or noble qualities). Black women fare no better in their casting as garish prostitutes, crude and harsh mothers, disrespectful and disgusted wives and a host of other dignity-denying roles.

Dr. Maulana Karenga, says the task is to reaffirm the need and the practice of Black artistic standards. Which encourage the highest levels of creativity, defend artistic freedom and insist on artistic responsibility in respect for the dignity and interests of African people and their right to freedom from any form of degradation or devaluing-artistic. After all, if not this, then what? And, if we don't respect, reaffirm, and liberate ourselves, and build good, dignity-affirming lives, who will?

The more our people become exposed to the negative images on television and the negative and non-encouraging voices on the radio, the more we will attempt to live out that lifestyle. We will start copying it and our peers will begin to follow. When our peers are engaging in such negative behavior, and no one is correcting it, it will make us feel that it's okay for us to engage in the negative behaviors.

If we see more positive images on television and hear more positive voices on the radio, we would be willing to engage in positive activities. If most of our peers begin engaging in positive behaviors on a daily basis, the less likely we will be encouraged to engage in negative behavior.

If anyone, especially another black person, freely fix their mouth to call another black person, "NIGGA," a name that's meant to make us mentally weak and dependent on white supremacy, they will dance freely in the degradation and dehumanization of our own people to please slave masters. They are collaborating with our oppressors plan to destroy the entire black race.

Let's examine the world we live in, that consist of those individuals, who are collaborating with our oppressors plan of destroying the black race.

- We are in a world, where our successful Black women envy our young black sisters, who are striving to walk in their shoes, because they either have lighter skin than them, longer or prettier hair than them, larger buttocks than them, or because they attract the men they wish they wish to attract.
- In a world where our children are suffering due to the lack of education and leadership of our parents.
- In a world where our adult males are afraid of taking on the responsibilities of being a man, a father and husband.
- In a world where our fathers spend more time in the streets, jails and prisons, than at dinner tables with our family, leaving our

mothers attempting to take on the role of a father which she cannot do because she is not a man.

- In a world where our brothers would rather pick up a gun to shoot and kill one another, and to spend the rest of their life in prison, then to talk it out. Killing each other as part of the master plan of our oppressor.

- In a world, where we don't think outside the box so we settle for being trapped in one.

- In a world, where the media promote more violence in the black communities than the success of our black people.

- In a world where our people are lost, where I'm trying to get us back home.

In this world, we, as a people, must correct these kinds of issues in order to continue our advancement. We must stop enslaving our minds and one another and start building up our minds and building up one another.

Sisters, you must relax the muscles in your face and smile at our young sisters who are striving to be beautiful and successful as you. Reach out to them and pull them up to where you are. They are in need of your direction and encouragement so, when they become you, they can reach down and help someone who looks up to them. Sisters, you must develop love for one another. If you do not love your sister, you do not love yourself.

Love yourself to the point that you can see yourself in someone else. Let's re-birth our young angels, so they can grow to become beautiful, successful and responsible adults.

Taking on the role of leadership is an opportunity for you to see your craft, gift and desires manifest. There's no happier moment or feeling than witnessing someone change their life around and become successful because they were inspired by you. Take this opportunity to change a life.

As much as we encourage our children to get an education, we as adults must continue to seek knowledge for ourselves. We can't keep the same mental capacity we had when we were youth and young adults. Our brain is too powerful to keep generating and processing the same thoughts. We have the power to unlock parts of our brain that we didn't know we can unlock, to achieve the things we desire. That's done by seeking knowledge. If we aren't educating ourselves and obtaining new knowledge, our children won't be inspired to obtain new knowledge.

Our children who witness our motivation to learn will become more passionate about learning. So, when you encourage your child(ren) to go to school, be sure to encourage yourself to learn and be willing to share with your child what you have learned.

Our children look at us as their leaders. Therefore, we must carry ourselves in a respectable manner at all times while we are in their presence. We must show and teach them morals that are valuable such as self-respect, respect for others, self-discipline, self-love, and love for all. We must be the leaders we wish to see in our children, so they can be the leaders they wish to see in others and in their own children.

Brothers, brothers, brothers, there is absolutely nothing wrong with living a positive and productive lifestyle, taking care of your responsibilities, being a great father, partner, and/or husband. Being responsible and loving men, make you more of a man than males who engage in violent and criminal activity. Your family, especially your children, would love and appreciate you more if you broke free of those modern slave chains and provided them with the time, love and affection they require. Make decisions that benefited them and not just you. They won't remember all the gifts that you have showered them with, but they will remember all the times well spent and all the times you left them to suffer.

Your family will never fully respect you for putting the streets before them, chasing fast money and staying out all night. However, they would respect you more for obtaining a job or business, and coming home at night.

If you put the streets before them, and end up serving a lengthy prison sentence for a crime you have committed, they will always hold that against you - especially your children.

They will blame you for not showing them what it means to be responsible, for not teaching them how to love themselves, for not showing them what love is or how to love others, and for not showing up at graduations and ceremonies. They will blame you for their neglect, abuse, mistreatment and so forth because of a selfish decision you made. Most importantly, you can't purchase love with money and gifts and you can't at all, buy back the time lost. That goes for women as well.

Brothers and sisters, we must understand that it doesn't make us less of a man or woman if we walked away from fights and altercations. Violence doesn't resolve conflict, instead it escalates it. Effective communication resolves conflict.

If you find yourself in a confrontational situation that is not calming down, the best thing to do is walk away. Come back later to talk it out after things are calmed down. Who in their right mind want to fight for the rest of their life besides boxers and UFC fighters? I won't go into where boxing originated. I'll let you do the research.

However, information can't be receptive if two or more people are engaged in a heated argument. The better individual isn't the person who throws the first punch and engages in violence, but the one who makes a sound decision to walk away from it. I personally would respect you more for walking away than to stand up and fight. That is, if fighting is preventable. If not, defend yourself to the best of your ability.

Your life is too valuable and you can't predict the outcome of a fight or the strengths and weaknesses of your opponent(s). You might mess around and get severely injured or killed off one wrong move or by someone pulling out a deadly weapon. That leads to another one of us injured, dead or in jail when the situation could have been prevented by either talking it out or by walking away.

Another thing, the streets are not the path to success. They will not help you obtain and keep your true desires. There's nothing valuable in that lifestyle. All there is drugs and violence. All the effort and energy invested in being a drug dealer or gangsta could be invested in your talents and skills that can open doors to a better lifestyle.

We must put our heads together and think of ways to better our communities, instead of tearing them apart. We must break the cycle of robbing and killing each other, so you don't have to spend half if not the rest of your life in prison, or so our families won't have to mourn for the loss of their loved ones due to street violence. Put the guns away, grab one another hand and pull yourselves together.

When violence in our communities is exposed to the media, folks are not just feeling sorry or feeling sympathy for us. Many are excited and laughing at us as well.

As men and women, it's okay to disagree and bump heads as long as we can reach an agreement and shake hands. As men, we must lead by example and protect one another as well as each other's family and community. The best kinds of men in the world are intelligent men. A dangerous man is not a man with a gun, but a man with knowledge and wisdom.

As a people, we would have many opportunities but we are not putting our brains to use. Instead, we are violating the rights of other human beings, which lead to death or incarceration. I can almost guarantee that, if we change our minds and our lifestyle into a more positive one, life would be better for us all. Many doors will open up for us and society will begin to look at us differently.

Sisters, look here, what I need you all to do for me, for yourself and for our human race is to uplift our brothers. Speak life into them. Encourage them to achieve something greater than their eyes can see. No more criticism. No more degrading our men.

We would rather have a woman who allow us to be the head of our castle, one who submits (in seductive ways) to us, who plays the role of a woman, who is not focused on trying to be ahead physically and financially. We require a woman who doesn't have an attitude of my way or no way, who is independent but doesn't battle us for control. We require a woman who doesn't get paid to collaborate with our oppressors in the belittlement and destruction of our mind and body but who is dedicated to building with us, learning from us, and who is dedicated to experiencing the joys of life.

Brothers, men don't settle for women who are against them. We settle for women who are beneficial to our growth and to the growth of the empire.

Ladies, we come from kings and it's time for us to be treated like kings. Nurture us and support us at our side.

Brothers, what I need you all to do for me, for yourself and for our human race is to respect, love, lead, build, educate, protect, provide and serve our women and children. Become leaders, builders, educators' protectors, and providers, both in the home and in the community. No more being disrespectful to our women. No more neglecting and abandoning our children. No more making selfish decisions.

Our sisters would rather have a man at home with them, one who protects his loved ones no matter what, who is dedicated to family, and who doesn't make a living by violating the rights of others or by poisoning the bodies of others for a few quick bucks. Our sisters would love to have a man who risks his life protecting his family, not by robbing, stealing, and burglarizing the properties of others.

Sisters, women don't settle for a weak male, you save yourself for a strong man: strength in mind, body and soul. Study animals. Female Brown Capuchins solicit exclusively the dominant male. This has nothing to do with the male's genetic qualities and more to do with their willingness and ability to protect children they father.

Gentlemen, our women come from queens and it's time they be treated as such. I discuss more about the relationship between men and women in Chapter 6.

Single parenting mothers, while you are awaiting your rightful man, find your son(s) positive male role models who are able to discipline in ways that builds good character and strength. Strength in mind, body and soul. Find your daughter(s) positive male role models who can teach her how to recognize genuine love and respect from other males.

Single parenting fathers, while you are awaiting your rightful woman, find your son(s) positive female figures who can show what genuine love, affection and attention is supposed to be like from a female. Find your daughter(s) positive female role models as well, who will be willing to reach out to her and push her to develop into a strong, beautiful, confident and successful woman.

Remember, successful men and women are the true educators in life and, without them, there is no direction. Without direction, there is no leadership.

Men and women, we must take back the role of leadership in our homes and in our community. Leadership and positive reinforcement must be implemented. We have to be more family oriented. Spread love, joy. Promote healthy relationships. Educate effectively, protect, provide, and remain in the home. We have to shut off the negative television shows, music, discard negative video games, and most of all, we have to be that dominated force we started out as kings and queens.

Are you someone who is so gentle and sweet to others, who does the right things but never seem to get rewarded in the end, who never seem to receive the blessings you strongly desire? If so, maybe you should try re-evaluating your surroundings. Clear up your circle.

Those people and things surrounding you could be preventing you from receiving the blessings you require and deserve. Those people can be your peers, family, colleagues, acquaintances, group members or whoever.

If someone or something in your circle has negative energy, brings others down and is discouraging them from doing something positive, they are pulling out the good in you, your positive energy, and causing you to not receive the blessings you deserve.

It's highly important that you clean up your closet and get rid of the people and things that have a negative impact on your life, especially if you plan on achieving success.

Author, poet, motivational/public speaker, Basheer Jones, once said, "If a rose stood alone in a garden of weeds, the rose wouldn't survive. The weeds would all work together to kill off the roots that's causing that rose to grow." As I mentioned in the introduction of this book, you must think of your brain as a garden. You must plant good seeds in it. Water it and keep animals and weeds out in order to blossom healthy plants, fruits and vegetables. You have to plant positive thoughts in your mind (subconscious) in order to develop into the successful person, you wish to become.

The creator isn't going to reward you with the blessings you require, if you continue to allow yourself to be deployed by the negative influences of other people. If you are in control of your life, you must act like it. If not, others are going to control it for you.

The creator isn't the controller of your life, He is the director of it. Which means, He will not direct you to a positive route if you aren't brave enough to get rid of people and things that aren't beneficial to your growth and if you aren't disciplined and confident enough to take the first step toward change. Sitting in your room, in your car or in a cell, with your face in your lap, praying for blessings and relief, yet not making an effort toward change will only keep you in the same predicament. You must build up faith, belief and confidence, and take the first step toward change, so He can direct you to the path of success.

I think of my life and environment as a fish tank. I've had many different kinds of fish living in my habitat. Some came and left. Some stayed put. Some were eating others to get to the top of the food chain, while some existed to look good but served no real purpose. I have had some guide me to safer areas of the tank, while others guided me and tried to keep me in the dirtiest and dangerous areas of the tank. I have had ones who fought hard to keep my tank clean, holding onto the glass, cleaning up my environment and remaining by my side during trials and tribulations.

When the time had come for me to clean my environment of unfit people, those who were around just for a season, who had used me to benefit them, who had belittled and discouraged me, they were put in the bucket and poured down the sewers and out of my life.

Remaining in my tank were algae eaters. Those algae eaters served its purpose regardless of how many times the water and its environment had changed. They fought hard to keep my system clean, removing waste from my environment and stuck with me.

Find you a support system who are like algae eaters. Don't think of them as being dirty and living in filth, think of them as being those individuals who will play their role of support regardless of how many people enter and exit your life. Those who will cross over the valley and back, to ensure you live the best life possible.

Brothers and sisters, do what you have to do now so you can do what you want in the future. Change start with self. It doesn't start with anyone else. Step out of your comfort zone, that negative mindset, that negative environment, that negative and unhealthy relationship and go receive your blessings. Surround yourself with people and things who will empower you on a regular basis.

Once you begin making these adjustments in your life, you will soon start to see your dreams unfold and things start to work in your favor.

People who uplift and inspire you to reach your full potential are the key players you want on your team and they will get you to the championship.

Be the change for yourself, your family and for society. Own Thyself!

> "Negativity is the cause of disease, destruction and disaster. Positivity results in production. The goal is to eliminate negativity from your subconscious mind, so you can enjoy a lifetime of happiness and joy."
>
> — *JAMEEL DAVIS*
>
> "I salute the divinity in you. I see your divine self only.
>
> I see you as God sees you, made perfect in his image and likeness. (Florence Scovel Shinn)
>
> My judgement is suspended. I love our Creator; therefore, I love me. Because I love me, the way He created me to be, I love you as you are.
>
> If I harm you, I harm me. He who harms you, harms me."

CULTIVATING MINDS TO OWN THYSELF

— JAMEEL DAVIS

"I conclude from my experience, that no matter how bad things get, any person who resorts to evil as a weapon against a brother or sister, counts for nothing in God's great plan."

— GEORGE L. MARTIN

Chapter Five

FINDING THE LOVE OF MOM & DAD

"Every woman is a little girl at heart and she is looking for the love of her father, and if she had an awful daddy that didn't treat her right, didn't treat her mama right, she don't know what it is like to have the love of a man. If you are brave enough and man enough to love that woman, she will come back at you with a love you ain't never seen before in your life. It's going to scare her at first. She ain't going to know what's going on because she ain't never had it, but if you are honest with her and patient, she will love you like you ain't been loved before."

— TYLER PERRY

"Human dignity is the foundation of conscience. Children who are loved and, in return, taught to love themselves develop this fundamental dignity and respect for who they are. This is why the primary lesson of education is love. The teacher must love children and we know that the first teachers are parents. Children must also be loved by anyone who takes on the responsibility of education. People who never discover their mission and fail to develop moral lives are the same people who never learned to love their own souls or spiritual core. The nature of that core is known through love." —Na'im Akbar

As children, we study the behaviors and relationships of our mom and dad, guardians, grandma and grandpa, and other couples we spend the most of our time around without even knowing it. We pay much attention to how they carry themselves, how they behave at home, how they behave in public, how they walk and how they communicate. We also pay much attention to how they treat one another when we are in their presence. We become fascinated by what our parents/guardians do around us, not so much by what they say but what they do. Mental notes on how they express their love for one another and how they express their love for us are taken and applied to the subconscious mind. Some of our parents express a great amount of love, joy, and affection toward us and toward one another while many others express anger, hate, frustration, abuse, neglect and/or abandonment. The amount of stepmothers and stepfathers we have had and the number of partners our parents have encountered during our childhood and adolescent years, how they treat and interact with our biological parent(s) become recorded in our minds as well. The behaviors and lessons of relationships, unwillingly taught by our parents, have had an impact on the relationships we have experienced and those we currently experience as younger and older adults today.

Children always mimic what their parents do, no matter how big or small. That's who they spend the most of their time with. Parents are their children's first teacher. When most children see mommy and daddy kiss, hug, and loving one another, they tend to kiss, hug and be affectionate with others. When mommy and daddy, grandma and grandpa, or other couples, fight and argue with one another, more often than not, the child who witnesses this behavior tend to become more aggressive and dominant toward the opposite gender. These mental notes taken during the early stages of a child/youth's life are often put into action when they become adolescents, and young adults.

You may attempt to encourage your child to stop engaging in such aggressive behavior or you may even punish them for repeated poor behavior and they may not obey. They may not listen to your commands or obey your rules because you aren't stopping the aggressive behavior you are engaged in, especially while you are in their presence. Even if they decided to behave while in your presence to avoid discipline, it is a high possibility they will resume the behavior when you are no longer around, when they are with people who will not discipline them.

The more children practice and engage in aggressive behavior, or witness others engaging in such behavior, the more active they become in being aggressive and dominant toward others. Their aggressive behavior may eventually transform into adulthood, where they will be faced with cases of domestic violence, felonious assault, rape or even homicide charges.

As parents and as adults, we have to lead by example in front of our children. We have to promote and practice professionalism and mannerism. Therefore, our children will be well mannered and disciplined when they aren't in our presence. We must watch our behavior while in their presence and prevent them from experiencing violence as much as possible.

A lot of attention is paid to the number of partners parents bring home to their children. If you are bringing multiple sleeping partners home to your children and introducing them to your children as your friend and they witness you kissing and loving all over your "friends," you may have caused a problem. Your child may have recorded that into their mental notes and may think it's okay to kiss and love on their friends of the opposite sex. You may instruct them to stop, or even explain to them why they can't do that, or even discipline them for engaging in such behavior but they won't listen because you continue to engage in such behavior in their presence. You should be instructing yourself to stop engaging in such behavior. Better yet, discipline yourself. Don't discipline or abuse them for a problem you may have caused.

When your children become of age to begin dating and having intimacy, many of their dates may be introduced to you and others as their friends, whom they will be sleeping with. All because of what they heard mommy and daddy say and do over the years, recreating the cycle.

Many children, adolescents, and even adults are often looking for the love of their parents. Regardless of how old we get, we will always have that little boy in us or that little girl in us, who will be craving that genuine love and affection that our parents gave us or the love and affection they have failed to provide.

A child growing up in a home with parents who love one another and settle conflict peacefully will more than likely share those similar qualities/ characteristics and become family oriented when they begin a family of their own. Time, love, and affection from their parents would have taught them what love is and how to love themselves and others. This child will most likely seek a loving, respectable and caring partner when they become of age.

Children raised in broken homes, where love and morals do not exist, becomes damaged inside. They seek love and being loved by others. Many children raised in broken homes do not grow to be loving, affectionate, or caring people. Many become very dominant, controlling, angry, aggressive, depressed and become distant when it comes to love and attention from other individuals.

If mom and dad didn't love and kiss on them, or didn't make time for them, it's possible that they would grow to be very distant from love and affection and wouldn't make much time for others, their children, and their significant other.

When love isn't being introduced in the home and children aren't being taught how to love themselves, many grow up losing respect for themselves.

Love is supposed to be taught at home by their educators who are their parents. Love is also supposed to be taught by anyone who takes on the role of educating. If a child has never experienced love from his/her parents, they risk spending the rest of their life searching for something they never had and do not exist because they were never taught what love is or what love feels like.

During their search, they become at risk of becoming emotionally, physically, and spiritually hurt over and over again because their parents weren't knowledgeable enough on the subject of love themselves to teach them what love is and how someone is supposed to express their love to them.

Their parents lack of knowledge of love results in them running in and out of relationships, having multiple sex partners, looking for the love they never had in all the wrong places because they don't know what it looks like or feel like.

Instead of being real men, learning to love women and encouraging other males to love women, the majority of men is disrespectful toward our women. They call them derogatory names and treat them less than worthy. The same goes for women. Instead of treating men respectfully and encouraging them to be the good men they have the potential to be, many rather call them derogatory names and treat them less than worthy.

Many women who have had multiple relationships, children and sex partners aren't "hoes, sluts, tramps, bitches" or whatever derogatory name you call them. They are little girls at heart, searching for the love of their father or for the love of a man. If the men in their lives treated them like queens, instead of like nothing, many wouldn't have to run in and out of relationships, have multiple sex partners or risk being called out of their name.

To the many young men and older men disrespecting our young ladies and women, if someone's daddy hadn't treated her mother wrong but instead loved her right and taught her how to love him back, her daughter wouldn't have to experience the hardship of finding love through all the wrong people.

A man who wasn't loved or haven't been taught love as a child, adolescent, or young adult may not know what it means to love a woman or what it feels like to be loved. This results in him searching for the love he is missing through multiple women he has had sexual encounters with. He is not a slut, hoe, or whatever derogatory name you call him. He is a little boy at heart, searching for the love of his mother or the love of a woman. He searches for that love in every woman he encounters. If the woman in his life was a nurturing woman and treated him like a king, instead of criticizing and degrading him, maybe he would stay and wouldn't risk searching for love through different women.

To the many young ladies and women disrespecting our men, if someone's mother wouldn't have treated his daddy wrong and hadn't ran him away, but instead have loved him right, taught him how to love her back, his son would have learned how to love and respect women from his father.

A little girl who witnesses her mother get abused, battered, or even raped by daddy or by another man becomes damaged for life. She grows older either, fearing all men, finding love by dating women or dating men who are as aggressive as their dad or the man dating and beating their mother. Some women would date these kinds of men because their mommy didn't leave that dominant and abusive relationship. Again, mental notes from childhood put into play during adulthood. Because her mommy didn't leave that abusive relationship, that little girl who is now a woman may believe in her mind that what she witnessed her mother go through is how love is supposed to be. "Mommy was slapped, beaten and raped and stayed with dad or that man, so maybe I'm supposed to be slapped, beaten and raped, and I'm supposed to stay with him." Or, "since my mom cooked and cleaned for her abusive partner, I'm supposed to cook and clean for my dominant, abusive partner, so I won't be alone."

It is psychological that what our parents experience, we experience when we become adults. The little girl who watched her mother get abused/raped repeatedly will probably be the same girl who grows up seeking aggressive sex over passionate, romantic, or [1]Afrantic sex. If she accumulates a ton of stress, she may seek aggressive sex to rid her of all her problems. The sex would only be temporary relief, just like an aspirin or Tylenol is temporary relief for headaches. The headache will eventually return and so will all her problems. She risks racing through life sleeping and dealing with aggressive men, who are only temporary pain relievers and pain builders for her load of stress all because mommy have failed to leave that dominant and abusive relationship and because mommy and daddy have failed to teach their little girl how to love and how to handle difficult men and disagreements between them.

---

[1] The art of expressing love and affection among heterosexual African descendant couples, in an Afrocentric way. -Jameel Davis

Ladies, it's important that you walk away from that abusive relationship now and seek help on finding true intimacy. Search for a partner that is dedicated to helping you become a better you and dedicated to loving you and treating you like the queen you are.

A little boy who witnesses his mother get abused, battered, or raped by daddy or by another man is also damaged for life. He grows older becoming more aggressive and dominant toward women, beating them or even raping them as their father or the man who abused their mother had done. He would date and prey upon weak women, abuse them and take them for granted. He would use anger and or aggression to get things to go his way because he has never experienced his abusive daddy or the man in his house show affection to his mother. He spends life disrespecting women and being distant from love and affection. The little boy believes what he saw his dad do or what he saw another man do to his mother is what he's supposed to do. "Well, since my dad slapped her, I'm supposed to slap women when they don't listen and when they yell back." That little boy who experienced daddy or a man force himself on top of his mother and aggressively have sex with her may become the man forcing himself on top of other women, seeking aggressive sex rather than passionate, romantic, or Afrantic sex. He would then race through life sleeping with multiple women, who are only temporary pain relievers and builders, thinking they will solve all his problems. All because daddy or the man of the house wasn't loving and affectionate to his mother and because mommy and daddy have failed to teach him how to love, respect, and care for women, and how to handle disagreements between them.

Fellas, it's important that you treat females of all shapes, sizes, ages, and races with the utmost love and respect. Be passionate with them, seek advice on love and intimacy. Seek a woman that's willing to teach you how to love and whom is willing to provide you with the love you require.

Forcing yourself on top of women and abusing them will result in a lengthy prison sentence or death. Don't throw your life away for a problem that can be cured.

The poor behaviors and relationships of our parents and other adults, and the involuntary lessons taught by them to us, could be the cause of divorce and relationships falling apart, individuals being single parents and youth birthing babies. We, as parents, must improve our relationships and behavior with one another so that our children can grow to have successful loving relationships.

> "Being able to shower your child(ren) with every gift they desire doesn't make you the best parent in the world. Being able to shower them with the time love, attention, affection and direction they require make you the best parent in the world."
>
> *— JAMEEL DAVIS*

> "The womb of a female was created to be loved, pleased and cherished. Not to be abused, damaged, and taken for granted."
>
> *— JAMEEL DAVIS*

Chapter Six

YOU'VE BEEN DATING WRONG, SO DATE RIGHT

"Don't put your child(ren) in danger for lust. Lust isn't more important than the safety of your child(ren)"

— JAMEEL DAVIS

Did you just experienced a breakup or divorce? If so, it's time to re-find yourself and find your desired soulmate. After a breakup or divorce, it's important that you take time off for yourself. Take off about a year from relations and relationships. I call this, "The Re-evaluation Period."

A year should be enough time to re-find yourself and to figure out what you are looking for in a partner. During your evaluation period, I want you to dig deep within yourself, to find out what it is you want for yourself and make it your goal to get it. Use this time to find self-happiness. Do all the things you enjoy and focus mainly on you, because your happiness reflects on everyone around you.

Your re-evaluation period will help you become more self-disciplined and self-confident. It will help you determine your self-worth, your passion and your purpose.

After you have become self-disciplined, have gained self-confidence, boosted your self-esteem, determined your purpose and self-worth, begin evaluating yourself for dating and your dating candidates. What is it that you are looking for in a relationship? In a significant other?

Evaluate yourself and people of interest like, recruiters do candidates interested in working for a company or employees looking to move up the ladder in their current organization.

The dating world can become very complicated, especially if you are a very busy and productive individual. It may be difficult to balance dating with your family life, personal life and work life.

Dating is very expensive in terms of time and money, with time being our most important asset. It can cost us a lot of time and money to invest ourselves in people who are unworthy of us. Due to that nature, I have created a dating questionnaire titled, "Brain Teasers For Singles" which can be found below. Like a recruiter conducting a job interview, these questions can help save time and money from unfit people. They can help you better understand yourself, what you want for yourself, and they can help you become that right person for someone else.

Don't be afraid to challenge your mind and the minds of those who are requesting your time. Use these questions to prevent people from wasting your time and money, and use these questions to help you learn how to love and appreciate those who have been broken.

Brain Teasers For Singles

Self-Questionnaire

1. Since you've been single for quite some time now, have you grown mentally and spiritually? Or are you still stuck in the same mindset from your last encounter?
2. What have you done to better yourself?
3. What have you learned about yourself?
4. How much time have you invested in finding the new you?
5. What have you learned being single?
6. What new things and ideas do you value?
7. How have you prepared yourself for the next available person?
8. What characteristics and/or values should your next partner possess that are of value to you?
9. What do you have to offer your partner besides the norm: sex, money material possessions and the ability to cook and clean?

10. What is the new mission for when you become part of a partnership?

Dating Questionnaire

1. Do you have a criminal history? If so, what were your charges?
2. (Ask for a copy of records: their criminal clearance and child abuse. You need to know what kind of person you are dealing with and whom you are bringing around your children if you have any).
3. What is your purpose in life?
4. What dreams do you have that you want to become a reality?
5. What are your short- and long-term goals? What are you doing now to achieve them?
6. What is your highest level of academic education? Do you plan to further your academic education?
7. Are you willing to broaden your level of knowledge? Are you willing to learn new things?
8. What are your strengths and weaknesses?
9. What is your most recent accomplishment? How did you achieve it?
10. What was your biggest failure? What did you from learn it?
11. What are you most proud of?
12. How supportive are you of your family and friends?
13. What do you value in life?
14. What do you value most in friendships?
15. What negative tendencies do you possess (example: jealousy, insecurity, envy, hatred, selfishness)? Are you working to get rid of them? If so how?
16. What qualities/characteristics should a guy/girl possess in order for you to date him/her?
17. What is your ideal kind of date?
18. How long before a kiss? How long before sex?
19. What qualities/characteristics do I possess that are of value to you?
20. Why do you want to date me?
21. What are your relationship goals?

22. Besides, sex, money, material possessions, and the ability to cook and clean, what else do you have to offer your potential mate?
23. What do you plan to establish within the first months of a relationship? A year?
24. What do you value most in a relationship?
25. What are your strengths in a relationship? What are your weaknesses?
26. How was your childhood?
27. Did you have both parents? If so, how did they treat each other? How did they treat you? (were they loving and affectionate)
28. Do you enjoy children?
29. How well do you handle conflict and disagreements?
30. Describe a time in a past relationship where you had conflict. How did you handle it? What did you learn from it?
31. How well do you manage finances on an individual and relationship level?

When asking questions on this level, it's important to pick out keywords that are of importance to you and only you. Not your friends or family members. Also, look for warning signs when they respond. Are they looking directly at you? Or are they looking away or looking down? Do you think they are confident in their responses? Do they sound depressed?

These warning signs, as well as their responses to your questions, will help you weed out unfit people. They will also prepare you to become a better person and communicator, in terms of helping and caring for people and for answering questions in return. You may know something or someone who can assist them in their area of weakness and they may be able to assist you in your area of weakness.

When evaluating your potential partners, you want to eliminate general questions like what kind of car you drive? How big is your house? What is your favorite food and color?

Those questions don't tell you enough about a person. We all need a form of transportation, a place to sleep and food to eat. Someone will always have a better car, home, and better food than us. You want to develop questions that will allow that person to open up and reveal more of themselves to you. Don't be sidetracked by material possessions, those may not last long. And if all the person has to offer is material possessions, he or she will not last long either.

Most relationships fail because individuals don't know how to date, giving up boyfriend and girlfriend privileges before an actual relationship and commitment. If they knew how to date the correct way, they would be more successful in their relationships.

There are four levels in a relationship: Dating, Friendship, the Relationship and Commitment. In order to develop a successful relationship, you must navigate through each level starting at the first level. You shouldn't proceed to the next level until both you and your partner(s) are prepared to proceed together.

The dating stage is the stage where you are getting to know one another. You are asking the important questions to figure out and to determine what kind of person(s) you are dealing with. In this stage, visits between parties may be limited and occasionally you may go on outings. In this stage, you aren't giving up boyfriend and girlfriend privileges. You are learning each other likes and dislikes, character traits, what makes them upset and happy, and you are learning about their goals in life.

Keep in mind, when you are in the dating stage you are not committed nor are you in a relationship. You are allowed to date as many people as you can handle, as long as you aren't giving up boyfriend and girlfriend privileges. It's good to have options until you pick the one(s) you would be most comfortable with. If a person cannot accept the fact that you are only dating and you're trying to find your soulmate(s), then they aren't worth dating. Instead of complaining, they should be putting in effort to win you over.

Once you narrow your potential partners down to a reasonable number and you all are comfortable with what each other have going for yourselves and what each have to offer, it's safe to advance to the friendship level and begin establishing a strong, genuine friendship.

While in the friendship stage, you are exploring each other's adventure world, your favorite places to go, fun activities, hanging out more, building trust, sharing secrets and helping one another grow. Still, during the friendship stage, you are not giving up boyfriend and girlfriend privileges. As I mentioned before, it's like a job interview, weed out unfit candidates until you find the best possible candidate for the position: Why should I consider you over the next person? How can you help contribute to my goals? What are your goals for us? How are we going to get there? Keep your eyes open and your ears open wider. Take notes.

Lookout for actions and listen out for false information and fairy tales. Effective observation is the key.

Proceed to the next level, The Relationship, when you have chosen one person (or more if you are polygamous person) and you are satisfied with one another, have developed love for one another, and when both of you have reached an agreement to move forward. It is not likely to work if the other person(s) is dragged into the relationship. If your friend isn't ready to proceed forward, be patient and allow that person to adjust. There is no rush and please do not try to force them. If he or she is forced, it can potentially push them away.

It's a good idea to wait a while before making an agreement of commitment because you want to make sure the both of you are working out well as a team, and that it's truly what you want. If it's what you both want, agree to be committed to one another.

Throughout the course of the levels, you will learn more and more about one another. It's impossible to learn everything about a person, you just need to learn enough to where you feel comfortable sharing your life with them. While in a relationship, you both will still be dating, you will still be friends and you will still be in a committed relationship. Remember to always make time for one another and to always date. You should look to learn more things about the other and suggest new things to try and new places to visit. Trying new things will help keep the relationship fresh.

While in a relationship, don't let your partner try and change who you are. Remain yourself and the person they fell in love with. If needed, you can make small adjustments to better the relationship but, if it doesn't have a major impact on the relationship, don't bother changing. No one in the world is perfect and no one will ever be 100 percent happy with another person. With some things, we can just close our mouth about and deal with it instead of over stressing ourselves, trying to patch up every little thing. Your partner is supposed to love you for who you are, not make you into something you are not.

Also, do not let your friends go. Find time for them as well, because you will need them. Choose your own friends, those who are beneficial to your growth. Your partner should accept your friends for who they are and not choose your friends for you. There's no law stating that all your free time should be dedicated to your romantic afrantic companion. Continue to do some of the fun activities you did with your friends, before you got into a relationship. Don't have a boring relationship.

If you attempted to navigate to the relationship level and it's not working, at least you have that solid friendship foundation to fall back on.

Women are more loving and affectionate than men. A woman knows how she want to be loved and treated, and it's important that she teaches the man in her life how she wants to be loved, instead of waiting on him to do something he's never going to do. He may have loved another woman one way, but the love he gave that woman may not be the love that you require. Every woman isn't loved the same.

Men require a lot of attention and love from his woman. He knows what kind of love and attention he needs and it's important that he communicate it with the woman in his life. She may have loved another man differently than you, and how she loved him may not be the love and attention you require.

Sex and the pleasing of woman is the nature of man. Any woman who isn't willing to feed the desires and needs of her man, may lose her man to a woman who will gladly cater to those needs. I'm not saying that sex is always the case but, when the time comes for it, he shouldn't be discouraged by daggering mood killers such as no, stop, or get off me, or whatever his woman chooses to come up with. Why be with a woman who isn't dedicated to catering to the desire of man and who is equipped with daggering mood killers?

Ladies, there's nothing more discouraging and displeasing to a man than a woman not allowing her man to please her. If you are not in the mood for intimacy and sex, kindly tell him that you aren't in the mood and that you will be ready later.

After watching Dr. Umar's "Message to Black Women," most men, successful ones at that, including myself, require a woman who has a strong feminine phenotype (mental and physical attractiveness), who act and carry herself like a lady at all times and who has self-confidence, along with high self-esteem. We require a woman who is a trustful companion, a confidant, someone who we can share information with, without her sharing it to others including her closest friends and loved ones. Also, we desire a female who caters to our sexual fantasies as I mentioned before, and who is a good cook.

If you develop all those qualities, you won't have to worry about him leaving. Failure to provide all, there's a chance he will have a woman who will make up for the area(s) you lack in. For example, if you can't cook, there's a chance he will be getting fed somewhere else. It's not always the case but, in most cases, it's likely to happen.

> A person may have all the materials and money in the world, but that doesn't mean he or she is happy or that they know how to love, or even care for you mentally, spiritually, physically, and or emotionally. Take time to know yourself and your worth, so you may express it to your future partner.
>
> *— JAMEEL DAVIS*

"Happiness is an internal state that only you can create for yourself", says Dr. Umar Johnson. **No one can make you happy but you.**

So, don't become involved with someone or get married to someone, who you think will make you happy, because they won't.

If you aren't capable of making yourself happy, there's really nothing anyone can do to help you become happy.

— *JAMEEL DAVIS*

DEAR WOMAN,

Sometimes you'll just be too much woman.

Too smart, too sexy, too strong, too bold, too beautiful, too real.

Too much of something that makes a man feel like less of a man, which will start making you feel like you have to be less of a woman to be with that man.

One of the biggest mistakes you can make as a woman is removing jewels from your crown to make it easier for a man to carry.

You do not need a smaller crown.

You need a man with bigger hands.

— *MICHAEL E. REID*

DEAR MAN,

Sometimes you'll just be too much man.

Too wise, too handsome, too strong, too confident, too visionary, too outgoing.

Too much of a man that makes a woman feel like she isn't worthy of you, which will start making you feel like you have to be less of a man, in order for the woman who lacks the ability to elevate to have you.

One of the biggest mistakes you can make as a man, is demoting your worth and potential for a woman who isn't equipped to wear the crown that matches your position as king.

CULTIVATING MINDS TO OWN THYSELF

You do not need to devalue yourself to be in the presence of a woman, you need a woman who increases your current value.

— JAMEEL DAVIS

Chapter Seven

THANK THE CREATOR FOR ALL OF OUR CIRCUMSTANCES

"The day you learn to turn every situation into joy, will be the day you find joy and happiness. Be thankful for everything, even the worse and difficult things."

— JAMEEL DAVIS

Many people, especially those who have experienced my growth from childhood to an adult, have often asked how was I able to transform from being just an ordinary boy in poverty, high violent, dominated communities in Cleveland, Ohio, surrounded by negative influences, to becoming the positive, successful and highly respectable individual I am today?

You would have to read my book, *How Success Became My Focus* to truly understand that transformation. But in short, I made the transformation to become a positive figure by constantly reassuring myself as an adolescent and young adult that I will not become a product of my environment and will not follow the crowd. I sat back and figured out what the norm was doing and invested my efforts and energy doing the opposite. I took the first step by changing the way I think and the way I behaved. I didn't settle for lack. I wasn't lazy. I wasn't arrogant. I didn't complain and I didn't blame others for my problems.

When the Creator saw that in me, He helped me develop my desires, faith and determination for success, and He helped me become a better me. Since then, I've put every situation I faced, that was beyond my control, in the hands of our Creator. The obstacles I have I faced, I thought of them as being just a test from our Creator and said to myself, "I'm just being challenged to see if I can get through it," knowing our Creator would not put something before me that I'm not able to handle.

Instead of beating myself up about something that went wrong or reacting negatively, I thanked our Creator for the situation at hand. We praise our Creator for all the good we experience, why not praise our Creator for the challenges placed before us? With that mindset, I was able to avoid, dodge, and push through every obstacle experienced. I knew deep within the challenges I face are part of our Creator's master plan to reveal its true love for me.

Putting all of my faith in our higher power and thanking the power for all of my circumstances has allowed me to move mountains and experience the joys of life. For our higher power is my supplier and there's a supply for every demand. So, whenever I'm faced with a problem, I put the situation in the hands of the Creator because I am divinely protected. I fully let go and let our Creator!

I borrowed this from Florence Scovel Shinn. "I put this situation in the hands of infinite love and wisdom. If this is the divine plan, I bless it and no longer resist. But if it is not divinely planned, I give thanks that it is now dissolved and dissipated."

It really made sense for me to thank our Creator for everything and to be happy when things don't go as planned, when I read *Prison to Praise* by that Merlin Carothers, and found that he too had to be thankful for every situation he faced in order for him to experience the joys of life. I thought I was the only one who thought that way. But, when I discovered that Merlin Carothers had shared a similar experience with his own personal God, I knew I was on the right track.

In *Prison to Praise*, during a small prayer group, Carothers was asked by his God, "Are you glad that Jesus died for your sins?"

Carothers replied, "Yes, Lord, I'm Glad." He was then asked, "Does it make you feel good to think of his dying for your sins?" Carothers replied, "Yes, Lord it really does!" Then, he was asked, "Does it make you feel happy to know that He has given you eternal life by His death for you?" Carothers replied, "Yes, Lord it does!" He then was asked, "Do you strain or try hard to really be filled with joy that He died for you?" Carothers replied, "No, Lord, I'm filled with joy."

Carother's God wanted him to understand how easy it was to be glad that Christ died for him. Merlin Carothers said, he could clap his hands, laugh and sing with thanksgiving for what Christ has done for him. I feel the same way about our Creator. Merlin said everything inside him had became silent during the prayer group and then his God spoke again saying, "It really makes you glad that they took My Son and drove nails into His hands. It really makes you glad, doesn't it? It makes you glad that they took My Son and drove nails through his feet. It really makes you glad that they drove a spear through His side and the blood flowed down his body and dripped on the ground. It makes you very happy and you laugh with great joy because they did this to My Son doesn't it?"

Carothers said everything became silent again and he didn't know how to answer. He eventually said, "Yes, Lord, it does. I don't understand it, Father, but I am glad."

His God said, "Yes, my son, I want you to be glad!

Now, this is where I said, it really made sense for me to thank our

Creator for everything and to be happy when things don't go as planned.

Carother's God said to him, "Now, listen, my son. For the rest of your life, when anything happens to you that is any less difficult than what they did to My Son, I want you to be just as glad as you were when I first asked you if you were glad Christ died for you."

Carothers said, "Yes, Lord I understand. For the rest of my life, I am going to be thankful."

I resonated with Merlin Carothers. I made it my duty to be thankful for the rest of my life and to be grateful and happy for anything that happens to me that is any less difficult than what they did to the son of

Carother's God. Though I'm not religious, but spiritual, I found truth in Carother's story. Being thankful for all of that I endure have allowed me to be the positive force, the successful, joyous, and motivated individual I am today.

You too, can experience the joys of life, if you condition yourself to put all of your situations that are beyond your control in the hands of your Creator and begin believing that he is your supplier and that he will supply your demands.

When we thank our Creator for all of our circumstances and put problems that are beyond our control in the hands of our Creator, power flows into the situation and we soon start to see change in and/or around us. The change may result in us experiencing happiness and joy in the middle of what revealed to be a heartbroken situation or the entire situation may become different. There is a great plan laid out for us and we cannot move forward to the next level until we joyfully accept our life, happiness and our circumstances, as part of the plan.

After looking over my left and right shoulder, back to where I came from, I realized that I was only inches from the ground, standing tall as the grass weeds. I was held captive in the darkest light for the longest. Today, I am standing tall as the tallest tree tops, looking over the horizon, over seeing my past, present and future. Every dream and desire are possible through faith in our creator.

Everything you fear now may have been created by white supremacy. Fear and God do not occupy the same space. When you grow to understand universal law, you will no longer live in fear and worry. I'm divinely protected and I have no fear or worry. I'm in great health and in great spirits because I believe in the universal Creator. I'm happy and protected. The universal Creator has protected many others, me included, and will continue to protect us.

I do right by others, and I treat others how I treat myself. I add value to all I come in contact with continuously and unconditionally.

If you live in fear and with worry, you are practicing the wrong faith. The universal Creator, the one who created our skin and hair, will protect and heal us from all if not from most of our pain, harm, sickness, diseases and so forth. Most of what we endure is man-made anyway.

So, when the time is right for you, I want you to take a moment and reflect back to where you have come from, all that you have been through both good and bad, and look ahead to where you want to go. The same faith and effort that got you to your good times and through your bad times will get you to your desired destination.

PLEASE LEAVE YOUR BOOK REVIEW ON:

AMAZON.COM

BARNESANDNOBLE.COM

"You don't need TV-Film-Radio to make a difference.

All you need is you."

—*JAMEEL DAVIS*

Be determined to have a decided heart right now! Successful people make their decisions quickly and change their mind slowly. Unsuccessful people make their decisions slowly and change their mind quickly.

Which type of person are you?

Not yesterday, not 15 minutes ago, but what type of person are you right now?

The weakness of an undecided heart will dilute your strength and power.

A decided heart, on the other hand, will move mountains.

—ANDY ANDREWS

Part of owning yourself, is understanding the world around you. You cannot deploy yourself in a world you know nothing about. You do not need to understand everything about the world, but you should keep a close eye on things and people that can destroy who you are.

—JAMEEL DAVIS

"I Wouldn't Be Me If I Only Did

What You Approved Of Me To Do."

—JAMEEL DAVIS

REMARKS FROM THE AUTHOR

1. As of right now, be grateful that you are alive. Life is the greatest gift of all. Nothing else truly matters.
2. As of right now, Love yourself, believe in yourself and express yourself in a way that shows good character, dignity, respect, strength, and confidence.
3. As of right now, begin eliminating your negative tendencies; jealousy, hatred, selfishness and envy. A negative attitude toward others will not foster your successful journey. You must show empathy, compassion and respect toward others. Also, be mindful of the words you use when talking about yourself because they may stick and become your reality.
4. As of right now, feed your mind healthy fruits and vegetables: positive people, books, music, television, movies, and so forth. Those weeds in your garden may prevent you from growing further. It's up to the creator to put you in a situation, but it's up to you to be brave enough to remove yourself from the situation. Prayer alone will not work. Prayer without work is void.
5. As of right now, stop living your life pleasing others. Live your life pleasing yourself.
6. As of right now, stop competing with other for fashion/material items etc., There will always be someone with more or less than you.
7. As of right now, stop depending on others for your success and greatness. Put in your on effort and go get what you deserve.
8. As of right now, every royalty you receive, rather it's a paycheck or donation, take out a portion for yourself and put it in a safe place.

9. Over time you will have a nice amount saved for a vacation that you truly deserve or for an investment of your choice.

10. As of right now, I love you and I'll always love you, for the person that you are.

11. As of right now, share this book with someone else or encourage them to purchase a copy. They may need it.

4 PLUS BASIC QUESTIONS OF IDENTITY

1. **WHO AM I?** -- What values, history, traditions and cultural paradigms do I internalize, employ, and continue to practice in my daily life?

2. **HOW DID I COME TO BE WHO I AM?** -- To what extent do I recognize, appreciate and understand those social forces and factors that have helped to shape and mold me into the person I am today?

3. **AM I REALLY WHO I THINK I AM? -- To what extent do** I have, understand, and reflect the cultural authenticity of my people?

4. **AM I ALL I OUGHT TO BE?** -- To what extent do I possess and conscientiously apply the traditionally enduring ethical standards and moral code which define and dictate my ever evolving self towards full membership within the human family and my ultimate cosmic purpose?

If you wish, use the notes pages in the back of the book to answer these questions

ABOUT THE AUTHOR

Cleveland's own International Speaker & Author Jameel Davis, earned his BA in Justice Studies from Kent State University in 2013 and has been employed at the Cuyahoga County Sheriff Department ever since. Later after being employed at the Sheriff's Department, he became an Agent of Change, a Speaker, Writer,

Poet & Author. Davis is a positive and highly respectable individual. He is a man of change, an encouraging leader and is committed to lifting others up and shining rays of hope throughout Cleveland and beyond. He is known for his educational seminars surrounding book publishing, dating and relationships, and his speaking appearances at schools and organizations.

Jameel has served as a panelist for Cleveland Clinic's "Youth Violence Discussion", as part of their safe summer campaign, and Kent State University School of Journalism's, "My Voice. Our Stories" community discussion covered by WKYC Channel 3. He is featured in the 10th, 11th, & 12th Anniversary editions of Who's Who in Black Cleveland, the 10th edition being forwarded by LeBron James. He appeared as a guest on WVON -1690 Chicago, Matt McGill's Morning Show, WENZ Z1079, KAZ Radio TV Network, VIBE105 Toronto and on many other radio platforms.

Jameel has been featured at many Barnes & Noble Bookseller locations on the East Coast, has traveled across the country and internationally to Toronto, Ontario, Canada, appearing with his books, "How Success Became My Focus" and "Cultivating Minds To Own Thyself." He has entered and won poetry slams and has opened up for and performed alongside of international recording artist, Andre Cavor.

He has been nominated at the 2015 Ohio Entertainment Awards and the 2018 Legend Awards for Businessman of the Year. Jameel has been presented the 2017 Inspirational Entrepreneur Award presented by the Ohio Entertainment Awards and the 2018 prestigious Eric Scott Russell Kindness award presented at the 23rd Annual Rescuer of Humanity Awards Dinner at Landerhaven back in January 2018. Jameel was the first of seven award recipients that evening, who left an everlasting impression in the minds and hearts of 650+ guests with his captivating acceptance speech and poetry presentation.

Jameel Davis, who was born and raised by a very young mother in poverty dominated communities in Cleveland, enjoys traveling, spreading his wisdom and enjoying life.

PLEASE LEAVE YOUR BOOK REVIEW ON **AMAZON.COM & BARNESANDNOBLE.COM**

Follow **Jameel Davis** On Social Media

Instagram: @CultivatingMinds_

Facebook: Jameel Davis

Facebook: Cleveland Author Jameel Davis, Cultivating Minds To Own Thyself

Twitter: OwnThyself

LinkedIn: Jameel Davis

MORE FROM THE AUTHOR

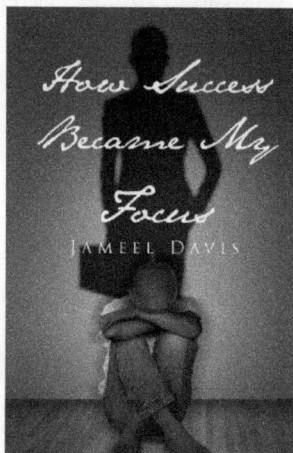

How Success Became My Focus - a gripping and potent story of shedding negative influences, hurdling obstacles and achieving personal success. How Success Became My Focus is a look at overcoming the obstacles that keep others from achieving their goals. Davis avoided many of the pitfalls that claim urban youths born to young mothers in communities plagued by high violence and high poverty in Cleveland, Ohio.

Readers who wish to experience this inspiring work, can purchase How Success Became My Focus at bookstores everywhere, online at the **Apple iTunes store**, **Amazon**, **Google Play** or **Barnes and Noble**.

www.PagePublishing.com/portfolio-view/how-success-became-my-focus/

ABOUT THE COVER MODEL

Braisha Owens is a designer of wearable arts and stylist for all, from the social misfits to the ultra-conservative. SHE is a model, creative visionary and entrepreneur. A dream promoter in her own right, she is DETERMINED to follow her dreams. Considering herself as an endorser of individuality and a lover of confidence, Braisha makes an effort to instill those principles in every acquaintance.

She created the concept for her business plan during the summer of 2013, which allowed her creative voice and love of individuality to blossom before her eyes. This gave birth to B.O.

Continuing to strive for the best and encouraging others to do the same, this is only the beginning for this young designer, stylist, and creative being. Her first stop was living in Chicago for a short time, next stop, who knows.

Though Akron, Ohio, have always been home, you can consider this young woman a traveling artist. With rebranding, she's pushing Kissed By BO, to be larger than life, or as she say, the world's largest runway. Kissed By BO, is where you can find the vault of her best work. Embracing her motto, can you rock a paper bag. Braisha desires for everyone to understand that confidence, should shine through any outfit. Armed with her faith in God, she carries a positive attitude and is definitely going places.

Follow Braisha Owens @kissedbybo on Instagram and Like Kissedbybo on Facebook

What Legacy Will You Leave?

What Will You Be Remembered For?

DEDICATION

This book is dedicated to the many individuals who are inspired by me and the work I do, as well as those who learn from me and whom I have encouraged to become their best self. Some of them are:

Jaheir Davis, Jason Daniels Jr., Tatum, Madison, Andre Kent Jr., Tahja Mosley, Aziah Chavers, Paris Tolbert, Bernice "Mama" Mainor, Alan and Arlene Williamson, Louise Davis, Jason Daniels, Janice Willis, Knokita Willis, Icesha Willis, Shavonne Willis, Ronald Mainor, Jayson Hawkins, Aaron Huff, Brittany Jackson, Alana Kee, Alfred and Helen Hudson, Aubrey Rose, A'bria Robinson, Robin Vandessppool, Trent Pryll, Ryan Wright, Angel Jacobs, Ishmael Dowdy, Teshawnda Wilkerson, Brooke Bishop, Jewel Daniels, JaReisha Gibson, Kevin Conwell Jr., Cierra Irby, Andrew Lloyd, Tira Heard, Aneshia Wilkes, Patricia Ballard, Leon Anderson, Walter Patton, Jonathan Rodriguez, Antwan Watson, Andre Russell, Anjeaneet Anderson, Su'Rai Burt, Cheryl Thomas, Jason Hudson, Amber Cannon, Cierra Hicks, Lashya Smith, Daira Smith, Jeremiah Kimble, Angelique Harris, Katrina Mardis, Shamonica McCall, Dameyonna Willis, Shanine Moore, Angel Norvell, Brittany Reese

ACKNOWLEDGEMENTS

One evening, while preparing for a 12 hour work shift at the County Corrections Center in Cleveland, Ohio, a colleague of mine Mr.Collins, told me he had brought in a book for me. He retrieved On Becoming A Leader by Warren Bennis from his gym bag and handed it to me. Upon expressing my gratitude, I read the acknowledgements and the introduction. It was the introduction of that book, that inspired me to write Cultivating Minds To Own Thyself. So, I give a special thanks to my colleague, Mr. Collins for thinking of me when he came across On Becoming A Leader.

I would like to recognize those who have supported me during the writing process of Cultivating Minds To Own Thyself. To my son Jaheir, who have inspired me throughout the entire writing process, who was up under me late nights and early mornings as I typed, anxious to be part of what I was doing. My loving mother Louise, my loving grandparents Alan and Arlene Williamson, who helped remove some of the load from my back as I completed the book. I would like to thank my mother for supporting me in all that I do, for nurturing me from an infant to a prince. I'm very grateful of her for being receptive of my thoughts and goals, and for pushing me to achieve all that I can be. I would like to thank the sweetest soul I've ever known, my grandmother, for always treating me as the man I had the potential to be, for her kind words and small tokens of love and appreciation.

I would like to thank my grandfather Alan, for serving his purpose in leading, educating, protecting, serving, and providing for the family. His role in our lives have benefited my role as man in my family's life.

I would like to recognize my friends and family who have supported me every step of the way during my journey of success. I would like to thank my great-grandmother, Mama, for all the love she has provided me over the years and for constantly reminding me how proud of me she is, and for always telling me she love me. I also would like to extend my gratitude to my Grandfather Gerard for providing me with the resources and information needed to elevate my mind on the history and culture of my people. I would like to thank my sisters Tahja and Aziah for being the best sisters their brother could ask for and for making our time spent together priceless. I would like to thank my little brother Jason for being one of my biggest fans. I'm looking forward to guiding him on the path to manhood. I would like to thank my brother Paris, for looking up to me and for his will to learn from me so that he can become a better man than he already is. I thank my cousins, Matthew, Donald, and Brandon for being the big cousins that I always needed. They have supported me every step of the way, through laughter and fellowship. I thank my Aunt T'osha, Aunt Janice, Aunt Sandra, Aunt Trina, Aunt Lue-Lue, my Uncle George, my cousins Shawn, Brittany, Shavonne, Joann, and my cousin Knokita for being a few of my biggest supporters and for always encouraging me to do better. I would like to thank my friends who are like my brothers, Jayson, and Gerrell, for staying true to themselves, our friendship and for reminding me of my worth. I would like to thank my good friends, Alfred and his wife Helen, Katrina, Latonya, Joseph, David Martin IV, Freethinkers Walt, my role models, Andre Russell and Leon Anderson, my colleagues at the Cuyahoga County Corrections Center and all who have praised and supported me. You have inspired me to become the great individual that I am today.

I would like to express my deepest gratitude to award-winning poet, motivational speaker, radio host and author, Basheer Jones and is current and former team members for allowing me to take part in the Cleveland Renaissance Movement to foster positive change in Cleveland, Ohio. I've always wanted to meet and work alongside of Basheer. I first heard him speak to 9th grade students in the Cleveland Metropolitan School District during my senior year of high school and was inspired to become great like him. Sister Joy, Sister Aubrey, Sister A'bria and Sister Jaileika, thank you for seeing the good in me, believing me, supporting me and for being that shoulder when I'm in need of a shoulder to lean on. I can always count on you ladies to ease my heart when it becomes heavy.

I extend my heart out to The Reel Initiative Organization, which is an activist inspired movement that believes strongly in community involvement and selfless acts of giving not only to the community but among themselves to inspire each to reach their full potential and to promote true leadership for the community. David Blunt, Niesha Blunt, Charde, Wynn, Angel Jacobs, Lashawn, Tia, and everyone else in the group, I greatly appreciate each and everyone of you for your continuous efforts and support for a brighter tomorrow and for standing in my corner.

Who's Who Publishing Company, honored me and over two hundred black leaders and professionals in the Cleveland area in their 10th Anniversary Edition of Who's Who in Black Cleveland. I was also honored in their 11th Anniversary Edition of Who's Who in Black Cleveland as well. Who's Who in Black Cleveland is an opportunity for Who's Who Publishing to afford a measure of recognition to the men and women who have made their mark in their specific occupations, professions, or service to others in the community. Who's Who states, "a sincere effort was made to include those whose positions or accomplishments in their chosen fields are significant and whose contributions to community affairs, whether citywide or on the neighborhood level, have improved the quality of life for all of us." I give thanks to Who's Who Publishing for recognizing my outstanding work and service I provide to the Cleveland Community and beyond. I also would like to thank them for inviting me to the 10th and 11th Anniversary Edition of Who's Who in Black Cleveland networking reception and book unveiling ceremony. The ceremony allowed me to meet and network with black professionals and it has inspired me to reach greater heights in my writing career.

I would like to thank the many organizations for allowing me to share their platform: Project Love (Mary Alice, Maurice Newman) for allowing me to be part of their Civility Summit at the Boys and Girls Club of Cleveland and for selecting me to co-facilitate the Debra Ann November Kickoff For Kindness Event held at Cleveland State

University Wolstein Center. Cleveland Clinic, for selecting me as a panelist for their Youth Violence Discussion Panel, as part of their Safe Summer Campaign, The Cardinal Nest Foundation for selecting me to lead breakout sessions on effective communication skills at their Youth Empowerment Conference, Spoken Soul, Social Society, and Chris Vada for allowing me to showcase my talent of poetry and products at their establishments, Pastor Humphrey and Deacon Humphrey of Imani Church of Christ for opening their doors to me and for being wonderful grandparents to my son Jaheir, Principal Dr. Erica Wigton and 5th Grade Teacher Mrs. Lewis of Canterbury Elementary School, for selecting me as their keynote speaker for their 5th grade promotion ceremony.

I personally thank Robert Kiyosaki, Robert Allen, Napoleon Hill, Warren Bennis, Merlin Carothers, and Na'im Akbar, for showing me how to reinvent myself. They are part of the reason I am the person I am today. I will never be able to properly thank my good friends and their company, Terence J and the Amp Society, Kevin Conwell Jr. and 3KP Marketing, Cornelius Beard and ABE Event Printing, and Brittany Jackson and Simply Nicole's Creations for going above and beyond with my media and marketing needs, ensuring that my products and services are properly presented and distributed. Also, ensuring that my events are well promoted and professionally ran. I express my deepest gratitude to my friends and followers on my social media sites: LinkedIn, Facebook, Twitter, Instagram, and Google Plus for their constant love, support, inspiring posts and comments.

I'm very grateful of those who have helped make this project possible. Those people are my publishing consultant, literary agent, and editor, Rhonda Crowder of Rhonda Crowder & Associates, my cover photographer Demetrius Williams, and my cover design artist, creative director Kevin Conwell Jr., who worked extensive hours day in and day out to get this book in your hands.

I'm thankful of life, a healthy mind, body, and spirit. I thank the creator for revealing to me my purpose in life and for allowing it to impact others in a positive way. I give thanks to the creator for blessing me with a support system and a beautiful family. I give thanks to myself for having the passion to love, support, and protect those I come in contact with. I give thanks for the ability to be determined, disciplined, confident, humorous, intelligent, and respectful. I give thanks to myself for seeing this project through from beginning to end.

Brothers incarcerated in jail and or prison, and those who are doing time in work release centers, who have supported my work and became encouraged by it to do well in life, I couldn't have completed this project without you.

I give thanks to my higher power for placing me in a positive living environment, for allowing me to have my finances in order, for providing me with an excellent education and good investment vehicles.

Every moment is an opportunity to become a better YOU to make a difference, to fall, to get back up, to rise, to fall again, to rise right back up and to be the best YOU that you can be.

—*JAMEEL DAVIS*

NOTES

NOTES

NOTES

NOTES

NOTES

NOTES

NOTES

NOTES

NOTES

NOTES

REFERENCES

Akbar, Na'im. (1999). Know Thy Self. Mind Productions & Associates, Tallahassee, FL

Allen, James. (2011). As A Man Thinketh. Tarcher

Andrews, Andy. American author of self-help/advice books and a corporate speaker

Bartz, Daniel. Your Next Job probably won't be advertised

Behind The Name: the etymology and history of first names. (25, July, 2015). http://www.behindthename.com/

Bennis, Warren. (1989, 1994). On Becoming A Leader. Perseus Books. C&C Associates, Wilmington, MA

Byrne, Rhonda. (2006 November). The Secret.

Carothers, Merlin., R. (1970). Prison to Praise. Carothers, Merlin., R. (1972). Power in Praise.

Corday, Barbara. American television executive, writer and producer mainly known for co-creating the television series Cagney & Lacey.

Hamari Web. (2015). http://hamariweb.com/

Hill, Napoleon. (2007). Think And Grow Rich. Wilder Publications, LLC., Radford, VA

Jones, Basheer. Author, Poet, Motivational/Public Speaker

Karenga, M., Dr. (2007 June, 07). Beyond Minstrels, Mammies and Mascots: Demanding and Practicing Respect, Los Angeles Sentinel, 06-07-07, p.A-7

Kiyosaki, Robert., and Lechter, Sharon. (1997). Rich Dad Poor Dad. Warner Books, New York, NY Kiyosaki, Robert., and Lechter, Sharon. (2000). Rich Dad's Guide to Investing. Warner Books, New York, NY

Martin, George, L. (2001). Faithwalking In Our Time. 1st Book Library.

Maslow, Abraham. Father Reaches of Human Nature

Nobles, Wade., Dr. Professor emeritus in the Department of Africana Studies, the School of Ethnic Studies at San Francisco State University and is the founder and Executive Director of the Institute for the Advanced Study of Black Family, Life and Culture, Inc. in Oakland.

Perry, Tyler. American actor, director, screenwriter, playwright, producer, author, and songwriter, specializing in the gospel genre.

Raskin, Jamie. Constitutional law and legislation professor at American University and at Washington College of law.

Reid, Michael, E. (2014). Dear Woman. Michael Reid. Philadelphia, PA

Rosen, Elizabeth. (2013, September 2013). Understanding how income taxes work. http://www.irs.com/articles/income-tax

Schwartz, Arlene. Arlene Schwartz Personalized Resume Services

Seven Reflections. (2015). http://www.sevenreflections.com/name/Jaheir/

The Carnegie Foundation. (2015). For The Advancement of Teaching. http://www.carnegiefoundation.org/

Who's Who Publishing Co. (2015). Who's Who In Black Cleveland. Real Time Media. Columbus, OH www.whoswhopublishing.com

Zaphiropoulos, Renn. Founder of Versatec